The Promised Mahdī عجّل الله تعالى فرجه الشريف

The Words of Āyatullāh Bahjat on the Spring of His Emergence

Compiled by Sayyid Mahdī Shams ad-Dīn

AL-BURĀQ

Copyright

ISBN: 978-1-956276-60-2
Printed and published by al-Burāq Publications.
Translated and annotated by al-Burāq Publications. Where needed, context and transliterations were added. Some minor edits were made to the translated text.

www.al-Buraq.org
publications@al-Buraq.org

First Edition | February 2025 | 15th of Shaʿbān

Duʿāʾ al-Ḥujjah | دعاء الحجّة

The words on the front cover are from Duʿāʾ al-Ḥujjah:

اللّهُمَّ كُن لِوَلِيّكَ الحُجَّةِ ابنِ الحَسَنِ، صَلَواتُكَ عَلَيهِ وَعَلى آبائِهِ، فِي هٰذِهِ السّاعَةِ وَفي كُلِّ ساعَةٍ، وَلِيّاً وَحافِظاً، وَقائِداً وَناصِراً، وَدَليلاً وَعَيناً، حَتّى تُسكِنَهُ أَرضَكَ طَوعاً، وَتُمَتِّعَهُ فِيها طَويلاً

اللّهُمَّ كُن لِوَلِيّكَ الحُجَّةِ ابنِ الحَسَنِ،

Allāhumma kun li-waliyyika al-Ḥujjati bni al-Ḥasan,

O God, be, for Your representative, the Ḥujjat (proof) son of al-Ḥasan,

صَلَواتُكَ عَلَيهِ وَعَلى آبائِهِ،

Ṣalawātuka ʿalayhi wa-ʿalā ābāʾihi,

Your blessings be upon him and his forefathers,

فِي هٰذِهِ السّاعَةِ وَفِي كُلِّ ساعَةٍ،

,Fī hādhihi al-sāʿati wa-fī kulli sāʿatin

in this hour and in every hour,

وَلِيّاً وَحافِظاً،

Waliyyan wa-ḥāfiẓan,

a guardian, a protector,

وَقائِداً وَناصِراً،

Wa-qā'idan wa-nāṣiran,

a leader, a helper,

وَدَليلاً وَعَيناً،

Wa-dalīlan wa-ʿaynan,

a guide, and an eye (watching over him),

حَتّٰى تُسكِنَهُ أَرضَكَ طَوعاً،

Ḥattā tuskinahu arḍaka ṭawʿan,

until You settle him on Your Earth in obedience (to You),

وَتُمَتِّعَهُ فِيها طَويلاً

Wa-tumattiʿahu fīhā ṭawīlan

and grant him long-lasting enjoyment in it

Dedication

The publication of this book was made possible through the generous support of our donors.

بِسْمِ اللَّهِ الرَّحْمَٰنِ الرَّحِيمِ
الْحَمْدُ لِلَّهِ رَبِّ الْعَالَمِينَ الرَّحْمَٰنِ الرَّحِيمِ
مَالِكِ يَوْمِ الدِّينِ إِيَّاكَ نَعْبُدُ وَإِيَّاكَ نَسْتَعِينُ
اهْدِنَا الصِّرَاطَ الْمُسْتَقِيمَ صِرَاطَ الَّذِينَ
أَنْعَمْتَ عَلَيْهِمْ غَيْرِ الْمَغْضُوبِ عَلَيْهِمْ
وَلَا الضَّالِّينَ

Please recite *Sūrat al-Fātihah* and ask God for the Divine reward (*thawāb*) to be conferred upon the donors and also the souls of all the deceased in whose memory their loved ones have contributed graciously towards the publication of *The Promised Mahdī (aj): The Words of Āyatullāh Bahjat on the Spring of His Emergence.*

We begin by giving all praise and thanks to God ﷿ for giving us the *tawfīq* to translate this book. He has guided us and without Him, we would not have been guided to the straight path embodied by the Prophet Muḥammad ﷺ and the Ahl al-Bayt عليهم السلام.

This book is dedicated to all the scholars, martyrs and believers who worked tirelessly to promote the pure Muḥammadan path, especially Āyatullāh Muḥammad-Taqī Bahjat قدس سره and Sayyid Mahdī Shams ad-Dīn قدس سره.

We want to also give our thanks and appreciation to all believers from around the world and acknowledge the team which helped al-Burāq Publications complete this work, spending countless hours to make its publication possible. Please recite Sūrat al-Fātiḥah on behalf of them, their families, and their marḥūmīn.

This book is dedicated in honor of the following individuals. Please remember them in your prayers and may God ﷿ have mercy on them and their loved ones.

SAKINA FATIMA HUSAIN AND HAIDER ALI HUSAIN
KINDLY REQUEST THAT YOU PLEASE RECITE
SŪRAT AL-FĀTIḤAH
FOR THEIR GREAT GRANDPARENTS

BASHARAT HUSAIN SON OF SHUJAT HUSAIN &
KISHWARI FATIMA DAUGHTER OF MOMIN HUSAIN

AKHTAR HUSAIN SON OF MOHAMMAD AMIL &
KANEEZ FATIMA DAUGHTER OF HAIDER HUSAIN

SYED AKHTAR ABBAS NAQVI SON OF SYED NAYYAR HUSSAIN NAQVI &
SYEDA TAHERA ABBAS NAQVI DAUGHTER OF SYED HADI HUSSAIN NAQVI

SYED SHAKIR HUSSAIN ZAIDI SON OF SYED MUMTAZ ZAIDI

We hope that you take the time to read this book to increase your connection
to God ﷻ, the Prophet ﷺ, and his Ahl al-Bayt عليهم السلام

Dr. Azmat & Sarah Husain

Terms of Respect

The following Arabic phrases have been used throughout this book in their respective places to show the reverence which the noble personalities deserve.

عزّ وجلّ

Used for God, meaning:
Exalted and Sublime (Perfect) is He

صلى الله عليه وآله

Used for Prophet Muḥammad, meaning:
Blessings from God be upon him and his family

عليه السلام

Used for a man (singular) of a high status, meaning:
Peace be upon him

عليها السلام

Used for a woman (singular) of a high status, meaning:
Peace be upon her

عليهما السلام

Used for men/women (dual) of a high status, meaning:
Peace be upon them both

عليهم السلام

Used for men and/or women (plural) of a high status, meaning:
Peace be upon them all

عجّل الله تعالى فرجه الشريف

Used for Imām Muḥammad al-Mahdī, meaning:
May God hasten his return

قدّس سرّه

Used for a deceased scholar, meaning:
May his resting [burial] place remain pure

Transliteration Table

The method of transliteration of Islāmic terminology from the Arabic language has been carried out according to the standard transliteration table below.

ء	ʾ	ر	r	ف	f
ا	a	ز	z	ق	q
ب	b	س	s	ك	k
ت	t	ش	sh	ل	l
ث	th	ص	ṣ	م	m
ج	j	ض	ḍ	ن	n
ح	ḥ	ط	ṭ	و	w
خ	kh	ظ	ẓ	ه	h
د	d	ع	ʿ	ي	y
ذ	dh	غ	gh		
Long Vowels					
ا	ā	و	ū	ي	ī
Short Vowels					
ـَ	a	ـُ	u	ـِ	i

Table of Contents

Prefatory Note 1

Poetry by Āyatullāh Bahjat قدس سره 1

Biography of Āyatullāh Bahjat قدس سره 5

- His Childhood 5
- Setting off to ʿIrāq 8
- Migrating to Najaf 9
- The Holiest Shrine of the Ahl al-Bayt عليهم السلام 13
- Illustrious 17
- Looking Forward to the Union 19

Biography of Sayyid Shams 23

Springtime 25

- Springtime 25
- The Peak of Ascension 29
- In the Friend's Orbit 40
- Visual Manifestation 44

Occultation and Difficulties of the Way 49

- Why Occultation? 49
- Problems With the Occultation 50
- Evidence of the Occultation of the Imām 51
- The Calamity of the Absence of Imām 51
- The Difficulties of the Way of Imām 52
- The Patience And Enduring of the Imām of the Age عجل الله تعالى فرجه الشريف 52
- The Imām of the Age عجل الله تعالى فرجه الشريف In-House Arrest 53
- The Lineage of Sufyānī 54
- The Mischief of Sufyānī 54
- Sufyānī Exists 55

The Events of Sufyānī 55

Freedom Or Islām? 57

Genocide Before the Reappearance! 57

Delay in Reappearance! 57

Do Not Revolt! 58

The Meaning of Those Vested in Authority (Ulī l-'amr) 59

Mischief At the End of Time 60

The Sweet Fruits of the Coming of Imām 61

Demolish And Rebuild! 62

The Condition During the Occultation 62

The Trial of the Occultation 64

Mystical Climaxes During the Occultation 65

The Duty of the Waiters 69

Duties During the Era of Occultation 69

The Office of the Imām of the Age عجل الله تعالى فرجه الشريف 70

Preparedness For the Appearance 71

Are We Truly Waiters? 71

Believing in the Imām 72

Faith in the Imām! 73

Perfect Belief! 73

Complete Presence of the Imām 74

Complete Following 75

Perfect Nobility of the Imām of the Age عجل الله تعالى فرجه الشريف 76

The Ways of Communion 77

A Strong Bond With the Imām 77

The Way To Establishment, Love, And Communion 78

A Seeing Eye And A Hearing Ear 78

Closeness To the Master of Time عجل الله تعالى فرجه الشريف 79

Maintaining Communion With the Imām 80

Necessaries of the Waiting 80

The Method of Concealing One's Faith (Taqiyyah) 81

Requirement of the Waiting! 82

The Friend of the Prince 83

The Consent of the Imām of the Age 83

Achieving the Satisfaction of the Imām of the Age 84

In the Way of the Imām 85

The Dissatisfaction of the Imām of Time 85

Neglecting the Present Imām 87

It Is Not Required That the Imām Comes! 89

Oppressing the Imām 90

We Have Tied the Hands of Imām! 91

The Watching Eye of God 92

Shooting the Imām! 93

The Signature of Imām of Time 94

Present Among the Mystics 95

The Effects From Du'ā' al-Faraj 95

The Sorrows of the Imām of the Age 95

Shelter For the Believers 96

Ardent Attentiveness And Turning (To Him) 96

Fearful Heart in Prayer 97

The Perfection of Man 97

Public Invocations 98

Reforming the Self Is the Symbol of Communion 98

Continuous Presence 99

The Veils of Seeing 99

The Most Vital Invocation With Outcome 100

Praying For Imām 101

Du'ā' al-Faraj—the Invocation For Humanity 102

Du'ā' al-Faraj—the Invocation For Afflictions 102

Relief From Calamities Through Du'ā' al-Faraj 104

Certain Outcomes From Duʿā' al-Faraj 105
Duʿā' al-Faraj 107
Invocation During the Pilgrimage 107
Conditions And Results of Duʿā' al-Faraj 107
True Invocation 108
The Paths To the Reappearance 109
Duʿā' al-Faraj 109
Repentance And Invocation For the Reappearance 110
Invocations During the Era of Occultation 110
Duʿā' al-Faraj's Results for Those Who Have Wandered Astray 112
Weeping in Rank 113
Complete Bond With the Imām! 113
The Attentiveness of the Imām عجل الله فرجه Towards the Shīʿah 115
The Green Island 116
Those Thirsty For A Bond 117
Special Attentiveness of Imām 117
The Support of the Imām of the Age عجل الله فرجه 118
The Imām in the Heart 118
Pure Heart 119
The Length of Al-Mahdī's عجل الله فرجه Government 119
The Books of Sayyid 120
Nearing the Reappearance 123
Near the Reappearance 123
Reappearance in A Few Steps 124
The Reappearance Is Close 124
Hardening of Hearts: A Sign of the Reappearance 125
The Time For Reappearance? 125
From the Signs of Reappearance 126
Fixing the Time of the Reappearance 127
Preparing For the Reappearance 129

The Knowledge of the Imām عجل الله تعالى فرجه الشريف Regarding the Time of His Reappearance....130
The Time of Reappearance 131
The Year of Reappearance! 132
Do You Know....134
Traditions in the Era of Reappearance....134
The Method of Victory....135

The Honor of Encounters 137

Announcing Encounter....137
Claiming Encounter....138
Seeing the Friend....138
Better than Encounter!....139
Oblivion From His Eminence....139
The Way To Encounter....140
Self-Reformation is the Secret to True Honor....141
Reform, the Condition of Encounter....141
The Youthful Face of Imām....143
Letter On the Command of Imām....144
My Coming Is Close!....144
Experience the Time of Reappearance....145
The Attendance of Imām At (Religious) Gatherings....145
Definite Encounter....146
His Eminence in the Gathering of Ḥadīth al-Kisā’....146
Kūfī Encounter....147
The Blessings of Reappearance....148
Encounter in Sleep....148
The Control of the Imām of the Age عجل الله تعالى فرجه الشريف....150
Encounter in Madīnah....151
The Imām of the Age عجل الله تعالى فرجه الشريف in the Viewpoint of Ahl al-Sunnah ..152
Du‘ā’ al-Faraj At Its Right Time!....153

The Mosque of Jamkarān 153
Attachment To the Imām 154
The Imām's Plea For Supplication! 156
The Instruction of Taqlīd 157
Waiters of the Reappearance! 159
Identity Crisis 160
Du'ā' al-Ma'rifah: The Supplication of Knowledge 163
The Blessed Du'ā' 165
Du'ā' al-'Ahd 173

Prefatory Note

بسم الله الرحمن الرحيم

In the Name of God, the Beneficent, the Merciful

Imām Jaʿfar al-Ṣādiq عليه السلام says:

ليست الحكمة في كثرة العلم، بل في القدرة على إيصاله بأقلّ كلمات ممكنة

> Wisdom lays not in extensive knowledge but rather being able to convey that knowledge in as few words as possible.

Āyatullāh Bahjat قدس سره was a fountain of wisdom, and his answers quenched every questioner's thirst. He always looked upon the level the questioner was on and answered according to his state, according to the prophetic saying:

كلّم الناس على قدر عقولهم

Talk to people on the level they understand.

Poetry by Āyatullāh Bahjat قدس سره

ستبزغ شمس الربيع شئنا أم أبينا،

وستكتسي الأرض حلةً خضراء

تتفتح فيها الزهور وتورق الأشجار.

إنه ربيع ظهور المنتظر...

الذي يملأ الأرض بقسط السماء وعدالتها،

ويفيض دفء الهدى على القلوب التي أتعبها برد الشتاء.

إنه دفء الحرية والسلام،

دفء العزة والكرامة،

دفء السمو وتكامل العقول،

دفء الحجة والوئام،

دفء تحقيق الآمال ...

إنه ربيع ظهور الجمال والملكوت.

The sun of spring will rise, whether we will it or not,

And the Earth will be adorned with a green mantle,

Where flowers bloom and trees sprout their leaves.

It is the spring of the reappearance of the Awaited One...

The one who will fill the Earth with the justice of the heavens,

And pour the warmth of guidance into hearts wearied by winter's chill.

It is the warmth of freedom and peace,

The warmth of dignity and honor,

The warmth of transcendence and the perfection of intellects,

The warmth of proof and harmony,

The warmth of fulfilled hopes...

It is the spring of the reappearance of beauty and the divine realm.

Biography of Āyatullāh Bahjat ﷺ

His Childhood

On the night of the 25th of Shawwal 1334 A.H (August 23, 1916) the home of Karbalā'ī Mahmūd was blessed with the birth of a child that later went on to win the hearts of millions of lovers of knowledge and truth amongst the Shī'ah of the infallible household of the Prophet, peace be upon him and his pure progeny. He came to be known as Āyatullāh Hajj Shaykh Muḥammad-Taqī Bahjat ﷺ.

The righteous, well-known and trustworthy Karbalā'ī Mahmūd from Fūman, in the province of Gīlān, named his new son Muḥammad-Taqī, inspired by an event in his youth.[1]

His mother's death was the first tragic incident in his life. Muḥammad-Taqī had seen his mother's affection for only 16 months, and her death saddened all. His older sister played the role of his mother from then on.

From his childhood, Muḥammad-Taqī had been in his father's loving company and he would see the enthusiasm for Ahl al-Bayt ﷺ emit from his father's heart, put to paper

---

[1] The elders of the town narrate that when Karbalā'ī Maḥmūd was suffering from cholera at the age of 17 or 18 and on the verge of death, he heard a voice in his sleep, saying,

> Let him go, he is Muḥammad-Taqī's father.

He recovered soon after.

and used as eulogies by the bereaved mourners of Imām al-Ḥusayn 🕮.

During those times, Muḥammad-Taqī, whilst in his father's loving company even at this very tender age, composed eulogies himself. He was attracted to this martyr of love and grief, and his oppressed Imām was placed in his heart from then until the end of his life.[2]

The mourning ceremonies of Imām al-Ḥusayn 🕮 from every corner of the city, turned Muḥammad-Taqī's attention towards the traditional school of Mullah Ḥusayn Ka'kabi Fūmanī, and placed him amongst the reciters of the holy verses of the noble Qur'ān.

In the peace and quiet of his surroundings, he was acquainted with the pleasurable call of '*al*-ḥamdu li-llāhi rabbi l-'ālamīn*a* ' (All praise be to God, Lord of the Worlds) and gave his tongue the fragrance of the verses of the Noble Qur'ān, enthusiastically memorizing some chapters of it.

However, his thirsty soul could not be quenched, and he made his way to the Islāmic seminary of Fūman so that the verses of the Noble Qur'ān, and the teachings of the pure Imāms, peace be upon them, could further soothe the ears of his soul.

---

[2] Imām Ja'far al-Ṣādiq 🕮 has said,

> Verily the Martyrdom of Imām al-Ḥusayn has put a fire in the believers hearts that will never be quenched.

In Fūman's lively Islāmic seminary where varieties of religious sciences were discussed, he met Āyatullāh Aḥmad Sa'idi Fūmanī, self-purified, a great man of piety and knowledge, a person he greatly benefited from and with an ineffable seriousness and insatiable spirit, he quickly learned Islāmic sciences along with a few Persian texts such as the *Būstān* (The Orchard), *Gulistān* (The Rosary) and *Kalīlah wa Dimnah,* and after seven years of continuous efforts, he was ranked among the top students of his master. Blissful moments during the congregational prayers led by Āyatullāh Fūmanī, were remembered by both him and his student.[3]

In Jumāda al-Thāni of the year 1348, coinciding with November 1929, it was time for Muḥammad-Taqī to migrate from home. Undoubtedly, the mentioning of the glorious Islāmic seminaries of 'Irāq during the solitary moments that Muḥammad-Taqī had with the scholars of Fūman's seminary, who themselves had been educated in Najaf, exhilarated his eagerness, and took his heart to the shining domes of the Holy Shrine of Imām 'Alī and Imām al-Ḥusayn عليهما السلام.

---

[3] For years, Āyatullāh Sa'idi Fūmanī inquired about Āyatullāh Bahjat from his father, asking,

> How is our classmate?

Setting off to ʿIrāq

Muḥammad-Taqī decided to migrate to ʿIrāq, longing to calm his restless soul at the shrine of the infallible Imāms, and quench his thirst for truth in the presence of great scholars of the Islāmic seminary of ʿIrāq.

Having seen his enthusiasm, his father sent him to Karbalāʾ with one of his well-to-do friends. On his first trip, Muḥammad-Taqī failed to leave the country. The border police did not allow him to enter ʿIrāq because of the absence of his parents. Although disappointed, remembering a childhood incident made him certain that he would go to Karbalāʾ. He later did so... kissing the shrine of Imām al-Ḥusayn ﷺ and smelling the blessed soil of Karbalāʾ.

At that time, Muḥammad-Taqī was around fourteen years of age and had gained an abundance of knowledge even before having reached the religious age of puberty.

Muḥammad-Taqī stayed with his uncle who was living in ʿIrāq at that time, and after about a year, he moved to the seminary dorm and attended school. The Islāmic Seminary of Karbalāʾ was filled with great scholars. During that year, Muḥammad-Taqī studied parts of Islāmic jurisprudence (Fīqh) and basic principles of jurisprudence (Uṣūl) and in his second year, he put on the sacred clerical robe in the presence of Āyatullāh Jaʿfar Ḥāʾirī Fūmanī and his father, who joined him in Karbalāʾ.

He spent four years in Karbalā' and with continuous efforts, acquired knowledge, and insight, along with self-purification, and achieved excellence in ethics under the blessed shrine of the Master of Martyrs ﷺ. Undoubtedly, the precious moments on the threshold of the Martyr of Love were far greater than the hours spent in search of knowledge.

Migrating to Najaf

It was time to leave the Islāmic Seminary of Karbalā' for the Islāmic Seminary of Najaf, home, and the holy shrine of the Commander of the Faithful ﷺ.

Najaf's renowned seminary, with a history of one thousand years, was home to many theosophists, men of knowledge and piety. A place of mystics for those in search.

Āyatullāh Muḥammad-Taqī strived with determination and courage, seeking the knowledge entrusted by the Ahl al-Bayt ﷺ in the Islāmic Seminary of Najaf. He completed the advanced Islāmic sciences with Āyatullāh Murtaḍā Tāleqānī, Sayyid Hādī Mīlānī, Āyatullāh Sayyid Abū al-Qāsim Khū'ī, Āyatullāh 'Alī Muḥammad Burūjirdī and Āyatullāh Sayyid Mahmoud Shāhroudī . He then began to study the advanced Principles of Jurisprudence (*Kharej-e Uṣūl*) and advanced Islāmic Jurisprudence (*Kharej-e Fīqh*).

To study these advanced lessons he sat on the footstool of teachers of Islāmic Jurisprudence (Fīqh), Principles of Jurisprudence (Uṣūl) and Insight of Ahl al-Bayt.

His favorite teachers included Āyatullāh Ḍiya ʻIrāqi, Āyatullāh Mīrzāye Moʻīnī and Āyatullāh Muḥammad Kāẓim Shīrāzī.

He also benefited greatly from the distinguished scholar, Āyatullāh Sayyid Abū al-Ḥasan al-Isfahānī in Islāmic Jurisprudence (Fīqh).

Āyatullāh Muḥammad-Taqī's creativity, intellect, and meticulous attention to his studies made him a renowned student, whose questions were regarded seriously by his professors.[4]

Besides Uṣūl and Fīqh, Āyatullāh Muḥammad-Taqī was interested in philosophy and rational sciences, for which he studied the books *al-Ishārāt wal Tanbīhāt* and *Isfār* with Āyatullāh Sayyid Ḥusayn Badkubi.

Teaching advanced Islāmic sciences at the seminary, and assisting the great Shaykh ʻAbbās Qummī (compiler of

---

[4] To honor his master Āyatullāh Muḥammad-Ḥusayn Na'ini ﵀, he said,

> Before I became of religious age, I attended his congregational prayer and experienced such a state that I had experienced only in the congregational prayers of Āyatullāh Saʻidi Fūmani.

Mafātīḥ al-Jinān) to compile the book *Safīnat al-Biḥār* were amongst his other activities.

This, however, was not all that he gained from the great scholars of Najaf's seminary. He attained new spiritual heights and mystical knowledge alongside his masters in 'Irfan.[5]

He was deeply influenced by two prominent figures, the first being the great scholar Āyatullāh Gharawī Isfahānī, also known as *Kumpānī*, who possessed a genius methodical and philosophic mind. In addition to the methodical lessons of his master, Āyatullāh Bahjat gained spiritual and ethical benefits, which became a part of his character. The second figure that left a great impact on Āyatullāh Bahjat was a unique mystic ('ārif) and seeker of knowledge, Āyatullāh Mīrzā 'Alī Qāḍī ﷼.

When Āyatullāh Muḥammad-Taqī entered Najaf at the age of 18, he found the teacher he was in search of in Āyatullāh Mīrzā Qāḍī—a mountain of Tawḥīd (monotheism) in the words of Āyatullāh Sayyid Khumaynī.

Although very young, he managed to finish the itinerary of the spiritual path and become the pride of others, and

---

[5] 'Allamah Muḥammad-Taqī Ja'fari ﷼ says,

> When I was a student of Agha Āyatullāh Kāẓim Shīrāzī studying advanced Makāsib, Āyatullāh Bahjat was in the same class. I remember well that whenever he raised a question Āyatullāh Kāẓim paid close attention to it.

attract his master's close attention. He was called the scholar of Gīlān.[6]

The peaks and valleys of life in Najaf al-Ashraf provided him with a golden opportunity for self-purification and self-discipline, but the burden of his studies and his endeavor in purification and self-discipline was such that he became ill. He would treat himself by traveling to Samarra, Kāẓimiya and Karbalā' under different weather conditions.

After sixteen years of living near the shining dome of the Commander of the Faithful, Imām 'Alī ؑ, and the Master of the Martyrs, Imām al-Ḥusayn ؑ, with an untiring determination to acquire knowledge and insight in the presence of the best Islāmic scholars that the seminary had to offer, Muḥammad-Taqī reached the stage of Ijtihād and returned home to Fūman.

In Jumāda al-Thāni of the year 1364 Hijri, coinciding with August 1945, after having reached the age of 30, on his sister's advice, he decided to get married.

After a few months in Fūman, Āyatullāh Bahjat decided to travel to Najaf after the month of Ramadan of that year.

---

[6] A part of the letter sent to his student Ilahī Ṭabāṭabā'ī by Āyatullāh Qāḍī reads,

> Agha Āyatullāh Muḥammad-Taqī Gīlānī has made great progress in his studies.

He decided to stop by in Qom to get his passport and acquire information about the Islāmic Seminary of Qom before continuing towards Najaf.

The Holiest Shrine of the Ahl al-Bayt ﷺ

In the month of Shawwal 1364 A.H, coinciding with September 1945, Āyatullāh Bahjat set off for Qom. During his temporary stay in Qom, he received a series of heartbreaking news. On 28th of Safar, a few months into his stay in Qom, he received the news of his father's passing. However, he took comfort in the knowledge that his father was happy and content with the path his son had chosen before he left this world. Then followed from Najaf the news of the demise of Āyatullāh Abū al-Ḥasan al-Isfahānī and Āyatullāh Mīrzā ʿAlī Qāḍī in Najaf, both of whom were revered and dearly loved by him.

These were two of his masters that he had the fondest memories of from Najaf. This news was one of the reasons he lost his will to go back to Najaf and decided to stay permanently in Qom, near the blessed shrine of the Ahl al-Bayt ﷺ and the Islāmic Seminary.

Agha Bahjat's presence in the holy city of Qom had an outstanding impact on his life as well as the lives of many others.

He attended the advanced classes of the Marājiʿ (Great Scholars) in Qom. After 24 years of its revival by Āyatullāh

Ḥā'irī, the Islāmic seminary of Qom had become a powerful seminary with the presence of distinguished scholars and mujtahids. Although Āyatullāh Bahjat was a mujtahid of the highest standard, he, along with Āyatullāh Sayyid Khumaynī, Āyatullāh Gulpāyigānī and a few others, attended the classes of Āyatullāh Sayyid Ḥusayn Burūjirdī and Āyatullāh Muḥammad Ḥujjat Kūh Kamarī out of respect to the elders of the seminary. He was among the best students of his masters and became one of the most important critics of the class.

At the same time, he would also teach Uṣūl and Fīqh that lasted for over 60 years, right to the end of his blessed life.

In the mornings, he would teach advanced jurisprudence (Khārij Fīqh) and in the afternoons, he would teach advanced principles (Khārij Uṣūl). To avoid publicity, he first chose to teach in seminary rooms, and then moved the lessons to his home. Later on, in 1398 Hijri (1978 AD), at the insistence of his students, he moved the lessons to the Fāṭimīyyah Mosque, where he taught for the rest of his life.

His regular Friday morning ceremony of Imām al-Ḥusayn ؑ was first held at his house and then was moved to the Fāṭimīyyah Mosque. Through heat and cold, health and sickness, he continued to attend the Mourning sessions of Imām al-Ḥusayn ؑ until the end of his life. He would spend a part of the summer in Mashhad and these ceremonies would be held there during his stay. His insistence on having these weekly sessions was due to the will and recommendation of his beloved teacher of ethics, Āyatullāh Mīrzā Qāḍī, who would say,

> Do not forget the weekly Friday ceremonies of Imām al-Ḥusayn.[7]

He would lead all daily prayers in the congregation, which included the attendance of many great-distinguished scholars that were prominent personalities in their own right. In the last years of his life, he would only lead the afternoon prayers due to sickness. The feeling one would have during these prayers could not be expressed in words and could only be understood by some of those who were among the crowded lines that stretched from the mosque to the alley outside the mosque, listening to his prayer recitation.

He continued his daily morning ziyārah (visitation) to the Holy Shrine of Lady Maʿsūma ﷺ, the sister of Imām ʿAlī al-Riḍā ﷺ, after the morning prayers and duʿāʾs until the end of his blessed life at around the age of 90. He would sit in a corner of the holy shrine and recite ziyārah and duʿāʾ.

Āyatullāh Bahjat also wrote books on Uṣūl and Fīqh but did not have them published. He did not permit others to publish them even with their own money, saying,

---

[7] Part of the will of Āyatullāh Mīrzā Qāḍī ؒ to Āyatullāh Bahjat read,

> Do not neglect holding the weekly mourning sessions of the Master of Martyrs. It will help ease the pain.

There are still many manuscripts of great scholars that need to be published first.

Some of his books include: *Mabāḥith al-Uṣūl*, A Commentary and Review of Shaykh Anṣārī's *Makāsib* completed the book until the chapter of business (*Mu'āmalāt*), *Bahjat al-Faqīhiyyah*, Book review of *Dhakhīrat al-'Ibād*, Book review of Shaykh Anṣārī's *Manāsik al-Ḥajj* (*Rites of Ḥajj*), along with books of couplets and poems.

Major books that have been published by the insistence of his students include the *Risālah Tawḍīḥ al-Masā'il* in Persian and Arabic, and *Manāsik al-Ḥajj*. These two books were published by a group of scholars that compiled his fatwas with his approval. One of his other books is his commentary on the book *Wasīlat al-Najāt*, written by his master, Āyatullāh Sayyid Abū al-Ḥasan al-Isfahānī ﵀. The first volume of this book had been published with his approval. There is also the *Jam'i al-Masā'il*, a course on Fatwas in Islāmic Jurisprudence, which was the result of 25 years of expertise in the field. This invaluable book came out in 1992 in five volumes.

His diligence and efforts for over half a century cannot be put into words. It is impossible to express the feeling of his followers through simple words when the biggest impact he had on others was through other than words. Expressing the new feelings in the state of worship goes beyond the scope of this brief biography. How can one introduce the students that spread out like branches of a tree in every direction, attempting to elaborate upon a part of his teachings? Words cannot describe the prayer lines whose breaths were taken away by one of his mystic sighs.

Illustrious

Undoubtedly, one of the outstanding characteristics of Āyatullāh Bahjat was his tendency to shun publicity and insistently attempt to remain anonymous. In his younger days, when he realized that his insightful questions in classes of the great Marajiʿ were giving him publicity, he stopped asking them. He did not insist on teaching either. That is why he never chose a fixed suitable place to teach. His attendance in the classes of Āyatullāh al-Burūjirdī and other scholars at a time when he was well capable of teaching the same courses was another proof of his humility and anonymity.

Although he was one of the best students of Āyatullāh Mīrzā Qāḍī and acquired spiritual blessings in his childhood, he never promoted himself, and always refused to talk about the mystical experiences he gained in the company of his masters.[8]

---

[8] One of his students relates that,

> In all the years I have been attending his class, I have never heard him talk about himself.

When he would speak of his masters, he had to reveal some of his own secrets, but he never used the word 'I' while speaking.

He also never had any ambitions to become a Marjaʿ Taqlīd (religious authority). Even with 45 years of experience teaching advanced Principles and Islāmic Jurisprudence, he refused to accept this position.

Nevertheless, after the demise of Āyatullāh Sayyid Aḥmad Khwānsārī and Sayyid Abū al-Qāsim Khū'ī, a large number of believers, as well as many scholars, pressed upon him to publish his Risālah. He accepted their request, but with the condition that the book should not have his name on the cover.[9]

It is obvious that this great man, who had devoted his entire life to God ﷻ, earned a lofty position in the eyes of his Lord, in return for his sincerity in worship and servitude to his creator, and by the will of God ﷻ, he won the hearts of millions of believers around the world without intending to do so. How can words describe this special servant of God ﷻ who won hearts by the heart, not by words!

---

[9] One of his close relatives was quoted as saying,

> Before the demise of Āyatullāh Arākī, when Āyatullāh Bahjat realized that the Seniors of the Hawza were going to introduce him as a religious authority, he sent a message showing his dissatisfaction with the announcement of his name.

Looking Forward to the Union...

The midst of May 2009 were the last days of his waiting. During his entire blessed life, and now with a fatigued fragile body and thirst-filled soul, he wished to unite with the eternal. Someone who was a righteous servant of God عزّ وجلّ and thought of nothing other than being a good servant of his creator all his life, the moment of leaving for his beloved was the height of all joys for this true ʿārif (Gnostic). The ninety years of spiritual and physical struggle culminated with a secure and loving embrace by his Lord. However, his peace and tranquility was for his followers, lovers and students, an endless sorrow and grief. Devastated, they came in masses to see, for one last time, his blessed luminous face busy in the remembrance of God.

Sunday, the evening of the 17th of May 2009 was indeed, a sad evening for Qom. When the news of the demise of this great religious scholar broke out, it spread everywhere quickly. At first, all were in shock, and then the whole city was in mourning. Once the news was announced by the news agencies, devoted followers from all over the country rushed to Qom. On that day, Qom was covered in black. Since Āyatullāh Burūjirdī's funeral, Qom had never witnessed such enormous crowds of people for a funeral ceremony.

The body of this old sage and mystic was put to rest in the Holy Shrine of Lady Fāṭimah Maʿsūma عليها السلام.

Now the silence of the Fāṭimīyyah Mosque is the cry of separation. Now the small wooden door near the window beside the altar, his lovers and followers' hearts can only imagine an old man walking through the door with his face turned down, his lips fragrant with the remembrance of God, his eyes wet with tears and his forehead illuminated by the effects of prostration.

In the solitude of this mosque if you now desire seclusion, you must turn your head and lend the ears of your heart to the holy shrine of Ahl al-Bayt to listen to the recitation of Sūrat al-Fātiḥah and Sūrat al-Ikhlāṣ.

Maybe once again the call of "yā sīn wa-l-qur'āni l-ḥakīmi" of the Fāṭimīyyah Mosque will enter the divine realm of Friday mornings, but his seat will only be occupied by his soul.

Biography of Sayyid Shams

Āyatullāh Sayyid Mahdī Shams ad-Dīn, known as Sayyid Shams, was born in 1958 in Qom. He began his theological studies at the Islāmic seminary (*ḥawzah*) at the age of 12. His father, Sayyid Ṣādiq Shams, entrusted his education to Āyatullāh Bahjat, under whom he studied closely.

He started preaching at a young age and has spent over 30 years traveling internationally for lectures and religious teachings. He reached the level of ijtihād but did not emphasize titles, leading to his continued recognition as Ḥujjat ul-Islām. His focus remained on scholarship, teaching, and public engagement.

Shams ad-Dīn has authored over one hundred books and articles and delivers lectures for a significant portion of the year. He has been trained in Islāmic mysticism (ʿirfān) under Āyatullāh Bahjat قدس سره and continued his studies under his tutelage in the field until Āyatullāh Bahjat قدس سره passed away in 2009.

Springtime

Springtime

While this book bears a different title, we have thought of it as Springtime, for the friend's reappearance is the season of renewal for humankind. With the friend's coming, we will behold the joyful springtime of creation—a springtime of religion, knowledge, perfection, natural life, and creation revived at the hands of the eminent friend.

As the command of realizing the creation from the Merciful's Throne of Lordship was issued to the celestial beings, and the life-giving call of:

﴿إِنِّي جَاعِلٌ فِي ٱلْأَرْضِ خَلِيفَةً﴾

﴿innī jāʿilun fī l-ʾarḍi khalīfatan﴾

﴿Indeed I am going to set a viceroy on the Earth﴾[10]

tingled in the ears of the heavenly creatures; those who knew nothing but loftiness regretfully cried out and brought forth the dark side of mankind by exclaiming:

﴿أَتَجْعَلُ فِيهَا مَن يُفْسِدُ فِيهَا وَيَسْفِكُ ٱلدِّمَآءَ﴾

﴿ʾa-tajʿalu fīhā man yufsidu fīhā wa-yasfiku d-dimāʾa﴾

[10] Sūrat al-Baqarah, Verse 30.

﴿*Will You set in it someone who will cause corruption in it and shed blood*﴾[11]

and showed their gracious innermost, saying:

﴿وَنَحْنُ نُسَبِّحُ بِحَمْدِكَ وَنُقَدِّسُ لَكَ﴾

﴿*wa-naḥnu nusabbiḥu bi-ḥamdika wa-nuqaddisu laka*﴾

﴿*while we celebrate Your praise and proclaim Your sanctity?*﴾[12]

But the Wise, who sits upon the Throne of the world of creation, revealed about the most sophisticated creature around the Throne and on the carpet of the creation's foundation, which is elegantly flawless, naming it man and human, by giving a fine and deep answer and splendidly calmed their worry by stating:

﴿إِنِّي أَعْلَمُ مَا لَا تَعْلَمُونَ﴾

﴿*'innī 'a'lamu mā lā ta'lamūna*﴾

﴿*Indeed I know what you do not know*﴾[13]

---

[11] Sūrat al-Baqarah, Verse 30.

[12] Sūrat al-Baqarah, Verse 30.

[13] Sūrat al-Baqarah, Verse 30.

And when the first link in the chain of the bringers of the spring received the science of spring with the words:

﴿وَعَلَّمَ ءَادَمَ ٱلْأَسْمَآءَ كُلَّهَا﴾

﴿wa-ʿallama ʾādama l-ʾasmāʾa kullahā﴾

﴿And He taught Ādam the Names, all of them﴾[14]

his intellect's capacity was shown like a shining shooting star for the unwitting in such a way that the gazes dazzled in amazement; the divine deputy was placed in his final station as

﴿مِن نُّطْفَةٍ﴾

﴿min nuṭfatin﴾

﴿a drop of [seminal] fluid﴾[15]

and so everyone honored and praised the Eminent Friend and the Almighty Creator's pearl of creation and honestly confessed:

---

[14] Sūrat al-Baqarah, Verse 31.

[15] Sūrat al-Ḥajj, Verse 5.

فَتَبَارَكَ ٱللَّهُ أَحْسَنُ ٱلْخَٰلِقِينَ

{fa-tabāraka llāhu 'aḥsanu l-khāliqīnᵃ}

{So blessed is God, the best of creators!}[16]

The climax and peak of this spring must be sought during the reappearance of the creation's spring. And when the reappearance occurs, the realization of the springtime of the Eminent Friend's wise creation will be beheld for as far as the eye can see, as well as how the spring will blossom man's and the creation's heart and soul in the splendid unique civilization through the coming friend, Imām al-Mahdī.

And this spring, full of elegance, prosperity, and light, will soon scatter the autumn's winter-like coldness and frost. The heavenly promise mediated by the revelations-enlightened Messenger will bring fruit shortly. How beautiful, celestial, and divine the creation's final grandness will shine, and how overwhelming and enchanting it will make the soul and heart of the creation's pearl and its foremost purpose!

Beautiful are also those guiding statements and enlightening words of the wise sage, the leader towards the inn of love and the intellect's and soul's maturity, who grants the souls cold by the autumn a gnostical intoxication

---

[16] Sūrat al-Mu'minūn, Verse 14.

and enriches these aspirant seeker's preparation and ability in the classroom of spring, and promotes the light through his bright and learning deeds and words. Be it so!

That which is written in this book, which lays in the sight of hopeful eyes fixed upon the fortunate horizon of the friend's return are sublime thoughts of mind and reason and words by the contemporary mystic and gnostic, the jurisprudent, philosopher and ascetic, the God-witnessing servant, the representative of the Eminent Friend's mercy, follower and righteous representative of the returning friend; Āyatullāh Muḥammad-Taqī Bahjat (قدس سره) and this is the smallest way to show gratitude and honor him whom with God's support have realized this work.

May it shine in your soul!

The Peak of Ascension

ʿIbād b. Kathīr al-Baṣrī narrated the following; he said:

> I asked Imām Muḥammad al-Bāqir (عليه السلام),
>
> > What is the right of the believer on God?
>
> However, the Imām turned his face away and did not answer. I repeated my question thrice until he answered,

> Among the rights of the believer on God is that if he tells that date tree, "come!" the tree should come.

ʿIbād said:

> By God, that date tree which the Imām pointed at started moving towards him. At that moment, the Imām pointed at the date tree and said,
>
> > Stay where you are as I did not mean you![17]

In the explanation of this tradition, there are a few points worth considering:

1. The Imām said, *"Rights of the believer,"* not *"Right of the Imām,"* which means that this incident does not exclusively belong to the high station of Imāmate; it includes whoever has faith in it.

2. The narrator's question was a summarization: *"the right of the believer,"* that is, the right is upon God. However, the answer of the Imām was: *"Among the rights of the believer,"* as in a part of the rights of the believer upon God is this ... which means that the right of the believer upon God is far higher than this, and he has mentioned only a branch and fraction from

[17] Saʿīd al-Kāshānī, *al-Kharāʾij wa l-Jarāʾiḥ*, p. 196.

Majlisī, ʿAllamah Muḥammad Bāqir, *Biḥār al-Anwār*, Vol. 46, p. 248.

among the rights of the believer, but as the level of understanding and spiritual capacity of the asker was not deeper than this, an answer like that was given. If a man like Salmān al-Fārsī or Kumayl b. Ziyād asked such a question, it would not be known what answer would be given!

3. The effect of words and the power of ruling upon nature, in mystical (*'Irfāni*) and philosophical terminology, the authority upon nature—which is among the gifts of a true gnostic—is not a divine gift to the believer so that debates regarding disparity and the like should be made, but is rather the fruit of pains, spiritual training, self-building, struggle (*jihād*) against the ego and resisting carnal desires.

Piety (*taqwa*) is vital to reaching such an elevated rank. That is why He said:

﴿وَٱتَّقُواْ ٱللَّهَۖ وَيُعَلِّمُكُمُ ٱللَّهُۗ﴾

﴾*wa-ttaqū llāha wa-yu'allimukumu llāhu*﴿

﴾*Be wary of God and God will teach you*﴿[18]

In other words, develop piety so that God will make you aware of the world's mysteries and nature's secrets, resulting in your authority over creation.

[18] Sūrat al-Baqarah, Verse 282.

And the remarkable point in the continuation of this delicate divine verse is that He ﷻ says:

﴿وَٱللَّهُ بِكُلِّ شَيْءٍ عَلِيمٌ﴾

﴾wa-llāhu bi-kulli shay'in 'alīm^un^﴿

﴾and God has knowledge of all things﴿[19]

So reflect and act!

When it is said that the right of the believer upon God is such and such, it does not mean that God is indebted to the believer! As He is the Creator and the Supreme Giver of blessings, all creatures completely depend upon Him. Rather, it means that the bounties and generosity of His lordship demand that He bestows rewards upon every (good) deed, and through His wisdom, He certainly bestows rewards generously. This is just as when He ﷻ says:

﴿إِنَّ ٱللَّهَ ٱشْتَرَىٰ مِنَ ٱلْمُؤْمِنِينَ أَنفُسَهُمْ وَأَمْوَٰلَهُم بِأَنَّ لَهُمُ ٱلْجَنَّةَ﴾

﴾'inna llāha shtarā mina l-mu'minīna 'anfusahum wa-'amwālahum bi-'anna lahumu l-jannata﴿

﴾Indeed God has bought from the faithful their souls and their possessions for paradise to be theirs﴿[20]

---

[19] Sūrat al-Baqarah, Verse 282.

[20] Sūrat at-Tawbah, Verse 111.

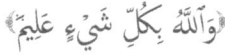

This is said even though the life and property of the entire humanity unconditionally belongs to the kingdom of God, and nobody has anything of his own:

﴿يَٰٓأَيُّهَا ٱلنَّاسُ أَنتُمُ ٱلْفُقَرَآءُ إِلَى ٱللَّهِ وَٱللَّهُ هُوَ ٱلْغَنِيُّ ٱلْحَمِيدُ﴾

﴾*yā-ʾayyuhā n-nāsu ʾantumu l-fuqarāʾu ʾilā llāhi wa-llāhu huwa l-ghaniyyu l-ḥamīdᵘ*﴿

﴾*O mankind! You are the ones who stand in need of God, and God—He is the Sufficient, the Laudable*﴿[21]

In the words of the divine sage Mullā Ṣadr ad-Dīn al-Shīrāzī, man's poverty is not accidental; rather, it is a part of man's essence.

> My heart is cut from the creations as all are in need. You are without need, and I seek refuge with You. In essence, we are poor while You are wealthy.
>
> This weakness of mine makes me show repentance

What is important is that if a man feels wealthy and without need, proud, rebellious, and ego-centered, he will cross the borders of suffering. The Noble Qurʾān says this:

---

[21] Sūrat Fāṭir, Verse 15.

﴿كَلَّآ إِنَّ ٱلْإِنسَٰنَ لَيَطْغَىٰٓ﴾

﴾kallā ʾinna l-ʾinsāna la-yaṭghā﴿

﴿أَن رَّءَاهُ ٱسْتَغْنَىٰٓ﴾

﴾ʾan raʾāhu staghnā﴿

﴾Indeed man becomes rebellious
when he considers himself without need﴿[22]

Those who have reached this lofty spiritual station and have been blessed with such an astonishing power would never reach there through their self-centeredness and egoism. The meaning of *"Be wary of God,"*[23] which is the first step and station in this celestial wayfaring, is the killing of carnal desires and passing by self-centeredness. These wayfarers give no importance to anything but God and His pleasure—such as disciplining the soul, rescuing those in calamity, or the like—and are only concerned with tasting the sweetness of God's proximity.

My father (Sayyid Ṣādiq Shams), may God have mercy upon him, narrated the following story whose source I am unaware of:

---

[22] Sūrat al-ʿAlaq, Verses 6–7.

[23] Sūrat al-Baqarah, Verse 282.

There was a man who was in a desperate search for learning God's Greatest Name (*Ism al- 'A'ẓam*), which is the key that opens the gates of the entire universe. After years of research and seeking, he found a sage of high rank who knew God's Greatest Name. He approached the sage and put forth and explained his desire to learn God's Greatest Name.

But the sage did not accept to teach him. He, however, insisted for a long time until the sage told him to go to the city gate tomorrow at sunrise, observe anything he sees, and then return and relate what he has seen.

The man did as he was told and stood at the city gate at sunrise, busy watching as he saw an old man leave the city to collect some firewood in the desert, packing it on his back and returning to the city to sell it. By the entrance to the city, the old man met one of the oppressive bullies who imperiously told him to hand over the firewood. The old man said,

> My livelihood is from these firewoods. Give me their worth in money and take them.

In a rage, the bully attacked the old man and, with force, took the firewoods from him as well as hitting and punching him—probably wounding the old man —and then left.

With sobs and moans, the old man stood up, shook his clothes, wiped off the dust, and went his way.

The man who was present told himself that if that sage had taught him the Greatest Name, he would have used it to uphold justice and defend the rights of that old man.

According to the agreement, the man returned to the sage and complained as he explained what he had seen:

> If you had taught me the Greatest Name, I would have saved the oppressed!

That great sage smiled and replied,

> The old man you saw is the same one who taught me the Great Name! But he did not use it for his prosperity! And you, who have little patience, how are you to store this great divine secret!

If we have heard that some of the friends of God apart from the infallibles have reached stations where they have access to "traveling through the Earth" (*ṭay al-'arḍ*) and "traveling through time" (*ṭay al-zamān*), it fits in the mentioned category.

The great ʿAllāmah Ṭabāṭabā'ī, said regarding his Master:

> Sayyid Qāḍī always had the honor to travel from Najaf to Karbalā' for Ziyārat. Never did anyone see him

travel by or sit in a car! And how this could be, no one knew! Except for one person, a tradesman, who had traveled to Mashhad and saw Sayyid Qāḍī in Mashhad. The tradesman put forth a problem with his passport, which he had, whereupon Sayyid Qāḍī fixed it and solved his problem.

When the tradesman returned to Najaf, he revealed that he had seen Sayyid Qāḍī in Mashhad. Sayyid Qāḍī became very angry upon hearing this and said:

> Everybody knows that I have been in Najaf and have not traveled anywhere![24]

Āyatullāh Muḥammad Ḥusayn Tihrānī ﵀, said:

> In Najaf, I heard from an Arab who was a wayfarer in the way of God and truly a lover who said: In those times when I was contemplating on the fascinating worlds, there was at times when a month or even more was spent with barely any food to eat. And we never felt this as time passed by! My family and I were never aware that such a long time had passed, and instead, we lived through it with much joy and happiness![25]

---

[24] "Mehre Taban", p. 287.

[25] *Al-Qiṣaṣ al-ʿAjība*, p. 236.

In any case, the proof of the reality of the spiritual powers which shine forth from a true gnostic is nothing but this luminous truth.

It is reported from one of the senior scholars and high-ranked teachers of Najaf that he said:

> I was in doubt regarding if the unveilings (*kashf*) and spiritual powers which were narrated regarding Āyatullāh Mīrzā ʿAlī Qāḍī Ṭabāṭabāʾī ؒ was true or fabricated. I contemplated this for long periods, and no one knew my thoughts.
>
> One day, I went to Masjid Kūfah for worship. Sayyid Qāḍī ؒ used to visit Masjid Kūfah often and had a personal room there. He also had a special bond with Masjid al-Sahlah, where he spent many nights worshipping until dawn.
>
> That day, I met Sayyid Qāḍī ؒ on my way to the mosque. After greetings, we proceeded until we reached the backside of the mosque. Once there, we sat down on the ground in the direction of Qiblah while leaning upon the mosque walls for some rest before we entered the mosque.
>
> We entered a deep conversation where Sayyid Qāḍī ؒ spoke about divine secrets and signs, the station of tawḥīd, and that unity is the reason for the creation of man. I was telling myself that if there truly is a reality

and we have not reached there, woe upon us! However, I still doubted whether there was a reality in this sense.

Suddenly, a large snake (snakes were common in those areas) crept out of a hole and started to crawl beside the wall towards us. As it reached us, I started to feel a tremendous fear in my heart. Sayyid Qāḍī قدس سره pointed at the snake and said:

> Die through the might of God!

and the snake became lifeless on the spot!

Sayyid Qāḍī قدس سره continued the conversation as if nothing had happened until we finally got up and entered the mosque.

He performed a two-unit prayer and entered his room, and I was occupied with my worship. Between my prayers, the thought of whether what had happened was real or fake and mere magic swiftly entered my mind, and I decided it was best to examine whether the snake was dead or had been brought back to life and crept away!

With these thoughts, I finished my worship, returned to the same spot outside the mosque, and saw that the snake was lying on the ground, lifeless! I kicked it, but it did not move! Upon this, I became very ashamed, and all my doubts disappeared. I returned to the mosque and continued my worship. After concluding my worship, I went to Masjid al-Sahlah and once again met Sayyid Qāḍī ﷻ there. He smiled at me and said:

> So dear fellow, did you examine as well?![26]

In the Friend's Orbit

The Imām of the Age ﷻ said:

فإنّا نحيط علما بأنبائكم ولا يعزب عنّا شيء من أخباركم

> We are aware of your situation, and nothing from your affairs is hidden from us.[27]

He who has constant control over all our affairs is "the watching eye of God" and is present among us, always sees us and witnesses our deeds. Now, how should we be?

A Sayyid narrated the following to the scholar of Qom, Sayyid Murtaḍā Ḥusaynī:

> In the night of a Thursday in the winter, when the weather was very cold, and it had snowed a lot, it suddenly came to my mind that it is the time when Shaykh Muḥammad-Taqī Bāfqī goes to Masjid

[26] Ibid., p. 43.

[27] Ṭabrisī, Shaykh Aḥmad b. ʿAlī Ṭabrisī, *al-Iḥtijāj*, Vol. 2, p. 322.

Jamkarān. I thought if only he could cancel his program for tonight and not go to Jamkarān!

My heart was really worried. At last, I could not endure any longer and went to his home, but no one was there, so I proceeded headlong to Masjid Jamkarān. On the way, there was a bakery. When the baker saw me, he said:

> Why are you restless?

I replied:

> I am worried for the Shaykh!

He said:

> Hours ago, I saw him proceed along this way, and you will certainly not reach him as he should be near Jamkarān by now!

I returned home and was even more restless. I occupied myself with prayers and invocations and could not sleep until dawn. My eyelids could barely stay open, so I closed them. I saw my Master, the Patron of the Age عجل الله تعالى فرجه الشريف. He said to me:

> Murtaḍa! Why are you restless? Do you think I am unaware of Shaykh's condition? I was just in Masjid Jamkarān and prepared his resting place!

On a similar note, Ḥāfiẓ has said:

> The Friend's beauty has no veil and cover but cast away the dust so you may see
>
> O heart, if you open your eyes to the light of guidance like a laughing candle, you will abandon the head

Any present-day industrial device and tool that works correctly has its described usefulness and value and is in motion in its specified orbit will undoubtedly lose its efficacy and might even be harmful if it is moved out of its orbit.

If we want to be secure in our movement towards perfection, the purpose of the creation, and not walk astray or be harmful, we must remain in "the Friend's orbit." He ﷻ himself said,

فإنا صنائع ربنا، والناس بعد صنائع لنا

> For We [the Ahl al-Bayt] are the creations of our Lord, and the people are, after that, our creations [through our guidance and teachings].[28]

The disciple of God, by the divine wish and will, is in movement. Thus, the disciple of the Imām of the Age ﷻ

[28] Ibid., p. 377.

must move in his orbit so that he will not be lost or rendered harmful by going out of the orbit.

The only criteria and basis to be in the orbit are to stay inside the circle of humanity, period! This is so because it is the human who circles the orbit of the Perfect Man and acts according to his will and satisfaction of him. It is the human who distances himself from egoism, carnal lusts, satanic desires, and whatever is in conflict with the spirituality of his Imām of the Time عجّل الله تعالى فرجه الشريف.

As a result, he remains on the path of guidance and prosperity. He continuously progresses on it to such heights that his potentiality completely connects to the peak of the orbit of guidance and reaches the climax of spiritual powers and perfections. He establishes a bond with the Occulted One عجّل الله تعالى فرجه الشريف and attracts his complete satisfaction. He is counted among the followers and friends or as one of his close companions.

Thus, one must find out his wants and move towards his satisfaction and will; so it could be said that one is successful and honored in observing and adhering to the divine command, that very prosperous command which is:

﴿يَٰٓأَيُّهَا ٱلَّذِينَ ءَامَنُواْ ٱتَّقُواْ ٱللَّهَ وَكُونُواْ مَعَ ٱلصَّٰدِقِينَ﴾

﴿yā-ʾayyuhā lladhīna ʾāmanū ttaqū llāha
wa-kūnū maʿa ṣ-ṣādiqīna﴾

﴾*O you who have faith!*
Be wary of God, and be with the Truthful﴿[29]

With the remark that in traditions, it has been narrated that the correct meaning of "the truthful ones."

Visual Manifestation

The skilled mystic *('ārif)*, the arrived wayfarer, the philosopher and jurisprudent, the prominent Master, the leader of the jurisprudents and mystics, his eminence Āyatullāh Muḥammad-Taqī Bahjat is without any trace of doubt one of these purified persons. It could even be said that he is among the leaders and pioneers of this group.

He was born 1334 A.H. (1915 A.D.) in Fūman (in Gilan, Irān). His father, Karbalā'ī Maḥmūd Bahjat, was from among the trustworthy and reliable persons, and because of this feature, people turned to him as an intermediate in their conflicts and problems. Apart from this, he sometimes composed skilled and deep poetry, which often streamed forth from his intense love for Ahl al-Bayt and showed the purity of his soul.

His eminence Āyatullāh Bahjat, may my soul be sacrificed for him, emigrated to the holy city of Qom in 1348 A.H. (1929 A.D.) after completing his primary studies in Arabic

---

[29] Sūrat at-Tawbah, Verse 119.

Author: *(ṣādiqīn)* in this verse is the pure Imāms.

grammar and literature. But he only stayed for a while in Qom and continued his journey to 'Irāq, where he settled in the holy city of Karbalā'. He seriously proceeded with his studies and purified his soul there for four years.

In the year 1352 A.H. (1933 A.D.), he moved to Najaf, where he for years studied under the renowned teachers of that Islāmic seminary (*ḥawzah*) such as Shaykh Ḍiyā' al-Dīn al-'Irāqī, Mīrzā Muḥammad Ḥusayn al-Nā'īnī, Muḥammad Ḥusayn Gharavī Iṣfahānī, whom he benefited from which made him reach high levels of knowledge.

His ethical and spiritual Master, who had a deep influence on his soul and conduct, was none but the matchless mystic and the ocean of gnosis and monotheism, his eminence Āyatullāh Mīrzā 'Alī Qāḍī ☙.

His eminence Āyatullāh Bahjat, may my soul be sacrificed for him, apart from jurisprudence and principles of jurisprudence, spent periods studying intellectual sciences and benefited from prominent scholars in this field. For example, he studied Ibn Sīna's *Ishārāt*, Mullā Ṣadra's *Asfār*, and similar works under the famous philosopher of that time, Sayyid Ḥusayn Bādkūbī, and became an authority in this field.

In the year 1364 A.H. (1344 A.D.), he returned to Irān, and after a short stay in Fūman, which only lasted for a few months, he went to the holy city of Qom. Once there, he reached the presence of the eminent divine sign and mountain of faith Ḥajj Ḥusayn Burūjirdī, where he completed his studies. Some think that his attendance at the lectures of the theological school of Qom was mostly due to formalities. This is so because, in Najaf, he dived into some of the renowned scholars' ocean of knowledge, and consequently, many of those who had attained the same degree as he depended upon reaping the harvest of his gnosis, jurisprudence, principles of jurisprudence, and philosophy!

His eminence Āyatullāh Bahjat, may my soul be sacrificed for him, has been busy for nearly 70 years teaching jurisprudence and its principles. He has trained leading, renowned, and prominent students who are shining stars in the bright sky of the Islāmic seminary.

His other endeavors include guiding disciples, polishing, reforming, and preparing them, writing deep and heavy works, and helping those in material and spiritual difficulties.

Worships such as recommended prayers (*nawāfil*), daily prayers and Ziyārat, fasting, constant remembrance and chant (*dhikr*), prayers along with intense weeping and crying, etc., and the like; worships which are well-known, general as well as specific, are all performed by him and are not needed to be mentioned.

Among his well-known characteristics are his Humility, avoidance of celebrity, restraint of desires, and disregard for the world and its vanities.

The beautiful bird of his spiritual powers, unveilings, mystical visions (*kashf*), and heavenly miracles is so phenomenal that this short introduction cannot adequately describe it. So leave this talk for another time!

May the munificent Lord prolong the blissful life of this extraordinary jurist (*faqih*) and let him live for as long as the sun of creation shines in shā'Allāh.

Wasalāmu 'alaykum wa Raḥmatullāhi wa Barakātuh

Sayyid Mahdī Shams ad-Dīn Spring 1384 (2005 A.D.)

Occultation and Difficulties of the Way

Imām 'Alī ﷺ said:

التاسع من ولدك يا حسين هو القائم بالحقّ المظهر للدين والباسط للعدل... ولكن بعد غيبة وحيرة، فلا يثبت فيها على دينه إلّا المخلصون المباشرون لروح اليقين، الذين أخذ الله عزّ وجلّ ميثاقهم بولايتنا، وكتب في قلوبهم الإيمان وأيّدهم بروح منه

> The ninth from your descendants, O Ḥusayn, is the Qā'im [the divinely appointed leader] with truth, the one who will manifest the religion and establish justice... but only after a period of occultation and confusion. None will remain steadfast in his faith except the sincere ones who are directly connected to the spirit of certainty—those whom God ﷻ has taken a covenant from regarding our *wilāyah* [divinely appointed authority], has inscribed faith in their hearts, and has supported them with a spirit from Him.[30]

Why Occultation?

The reason for the occultation of the Imām of Time ﷺ is we! If not, then who will kill him if he reappears? Is it the djinn who will kill that holy person? Or is man his assassin? We have answered in advance how we are going to protect and obey Imām, or we will murder him! The lowliness and backwardness of man are to such extent that the people of

---

[30] *Mu'jam Aḥadīth al-Imām al-Mahdī* ﷺ, Vol. 3, p. 402.

Prophet Ṣāliḥ ﷺ turned their backs to the camel of Ṣāliḥ ﷺ, even though it was a source of blessings and provision for them in a way which the Noble Qur'ān describes in the following words:

﴿لَّهَا شِرْبٌ وَلَكُمْ شِرْبُ يَوْمٍ مَّعْلُومٍ﴾

﴿lahā shirbun wa-lakum shirbu yawmin ma'lūmin﴾

﴿she shall drink and you shall drink on known days﴾[31]

Thus, just in the way that they destroyed their treasury of blessings and provisions by killing Ṣāliḥ's ﷺ camel as it was descending from the mountain, the possibility exists that we intellectual humans also kill the Imām of Time ﷻ for our interests, even though all bounties come through him, who certainly is way higher in grace than the camel of Ṣāliḥ ﷺ.[32]

Problems With the Occultation

Remarkable are those who do not believe in the Imāmate of the Imāms ﷺ and say:

> Why do you Shī'ah have faith in the leadership of such individuals who are not present among you to enjoy

[31] Sūrat ash-Shu'arā', Verse 155.

[32] *M'ālim al-Huda*, p. 41.

good and forbid evil *(al-Amr bil-Maʿrūf wal-Nahy ʿanil-Munkar)*?.

We say:

> When the Imāms عليهم السلام were among the people, their words and speeches had no esteem and validity amid your leaders![33]

Evidence of the Occultation of the Imām

The tradition of the two weighty things (*Ḥadīth al-Thaqalayn*) is among the arguments for proving the occultation of the Imām of Time عجل الله تعالى فرجه الشريف. In that tradition, it is said that the Qurʾān and Ahl al-Bayt will not be separated from each other—independent of whether they are present or absent!

The concept of occultation (*ghayba*) will become very clear if someone analyzes and studies the meaning of this tradition since otherwise, the prerequisite would be a separation of the Qurʾān and Ahl al-Bayt عليهم السلام.[34]

The Calamity of the Absence of Imām

The meaning of calamity in faith—when it is said, *Do not put calamity in our religion*—is the very same calamity we

---

[33] *Fī Riḥāb al-Shaykh Bahjat,* Vol. 1, p. 79.

[34] Ibid., p. 69.

currently are afflicted with, the absence of the Imām عجل الله تعالى فرجه الشريف! Which calamity is bigger than this?

God knows what bereavement we have due to this calamity. Especially considering that calamity in faith also causes worldly calamities—not vice versa![35]

The Difficulties of the Way of Imām

If we, like Imām al-Mahdī عجل الله تعالى فرجه الشريف, to our utmost capabilities, strive and work for the guidance of people, is it possible that we will not receive the attention and favor of the watching eye of God—the Imām of Time عجل الله تعالى فرجه الشريف? If we are on the path of that holiness and get mocked and scorned due to this, we should not become sad, and even so, we should proceed on the way of Truth with firm steps and show endurance and patience towards the harshness that faces us.[36]

The Patience And Enduring of the Imām of the Age عجل الله تعالى فرجه الشريف

Despite what great love we bear towards the Imām of Time عجل الله تعالى فرجه الشريف, is his reappearance not actualized by the talks of this servant or you (the reader)?

---

[35] Ibid., Vol. 2, p. 217.

[36] *M'ālim al-Huda*, p. 43.

They advised Imām ʿAlī to get on friendly terms with Muʿāwīya. If it was meant that he should listen to those talks, he would have done so right from the start. They told him to make peace and continue the war once his governance was firmly fixed, but Imām did not listen.

What patience God has given to the Occulted One! Thousand years have passed where day upon day, he witnesses what calamities befall the Muslims and what calamities the Muslims cast upon each other. And he endures it all![37]

The Imām of the Age In-House Arrest

How low our belief is and how high the belief of the Imām of Time is! That is if we are not counted as infidels in his eyes!

Why have we tied his hands, put him under house arrest, and will not even allow him to show himself?

Someone said: why do you pray for hastening of the reappearance? Is it that you want him to come so you can kill him? Most certainly, he will be a hindrance to your governments and rulings! Those who killed the rest of the Imāms were not crazy; rather, it was due to their ungodliness. Has the situation today supposedly changed?

---

[37] *Fī Riḥāb al-Shaykh Bahjat*, Vol 1, p. 123.

The Shaykhs of Islām said: the support for the caliph is unnecessary! I seek refuge in God from this, but it means that the Messenger of God ﷺ spoke meaninglessly! With this method, they shut his mouth and did not allow him to speak. They exclaimed,

> The Messenger of God ﷺ left the world and did not appoint a succeeding caliph![38]

The Lineage of Sufyānī

Recently, I saw in one of Ahl al-Sunnah's books that the lineage of Sufyānī does not reach Abū Sufiyan through Yazīd and Mu'āwīya but rather through one of the brothers of Mu'āwīya.

Likewise, in that book, it was written that when Sufyānī comes, he will kill everyone who is named Muḥammad, 'Alī, Ḥasan, Ḥusayn, Zaynab, and Umm Kulthūm, as well as a great number of pregnant women.[39]

The Mischief of Sufyānī

Do we have the strength to endure the killings of every 'Alī, Zaynab, and the like at five places where Sufyānī will reign, considering that they will say: why are we to be blamed

[38] Ibid., Vol. 2, p. 205.

[39] Ibid., Vol. 1, p. 186.

when it is our parent's fault who named us Ḥasan and ʿAlī? This condition will continue for eight months.[40]

Sufyānī Exists

Muqaddas Mashhadī 🕮, during a Ziyārah[41], asked God whether Sufyānī existed. At al-Kāẓimiyyah, in a transport vehicle, an Arab was sitting beside him. When the Arab stepped out of the car, he told him,

Yes, Sufyānī exists!

This happened five or six years ago.[42]

The Events of Sufyānī

I hope these hardships, sufferings, and afflictions for the Shīʿah will end. A multitude of narrations reports what oppression and tyranny Sufyānī will spread. The narrations are from Imām ʿAlī 🕮.

---

[40] Ibid., Vol. 2, p. 63.

[41] The term *ziyārah* means "visiting someone," but this visitation does not necessarily have to be physical. It can also refer to a spiritual ziyārah, such as sending peace and greetings to the Prophet 🕮 from afar. A physical ziyārah, on the other hand, involves visiting the Prophet's 🕮 grave in Madīnah. Depending on the context, ziyārah may be translated as "visitation" or left untranslated to preserve its specific devotional and spiritual connotation.

[42] Ibid., p. 421.

In a narration from Shīʿah sources, it has come that the reign of Sufyānī will not last for more than about eight months. However, during this short period, he will waste important resources and kill whoever is named Muḥammad, ʿAlī, Ḥasan, Ḥusayn, ʿĀtikah, and Umm Kulthūm. Then a number will tell him: our parents were sinners who named us Muḥammad, ʿAlī, and the like; we are not to be blamed! So he will give the order to kill just those who are named Ḥasan and Ḥusayn while releasing the others.

Ḥajj Nūrī narrates:

> Sufyānī will be taken to his eminence Patron of the Age in a state where his turban is wrapped around his neck. He will say to Imām:
>
> > O Son of the Messenger of God! Do not kill me!
>
> According to this narration, the bystanders will say:
>
> > Will you release someone who has killed so many from the descendants of the Messenger of God?!

They will pressure Imām to such an extent that he will tell them: do whatever you find is fit, you choose—do whatever you wish. In this way, Imām will give permission for his death where they conclusively will execute him.[43]

---

[43] Ibid., p. 84.

Freedom Or Islām?

During tumult in Irān, Manṣūr said openly in the parliament *(majlis)*:

> We want to remove Islām as the official religion.

The representatives in the parliament remained silent, and when he saw that they did not support his statement, he said,

> I mean that it should be freedom, with or without Islām!

It was not long until they killed that wicked person.

Genocide Before the Reappearance!

Some think that genocide will become a fact when Imām reappears! But it will not be such; rather, the killings will happen before the merge of Imām. In a narration, it has come that Sufyānī will kill 170,000 persons in such and such a place in ʿIrāq.[44]

Delay in Reappearance!

At the time when the wearing of the veil *(hijab)* was prohibited (in Irān), a person went into seclusion for the

[44] Ibid., p. 101.

overthrow of Pahlavī. Scholars came one after another to him and said:

> Mister!
>
> Do not continue this; the reappearance will be postponed!

This continued until two persons brought a third person as an intermediate to him, lifted him by the shoulders, and brought him with them. From a worldly perspective, the rank of those two persons was higher than the third one (the intermediate), who was also under the authority of those two persons. However, the situation was the opposite in that (unseen) world.[45]

Do Not Revolt!

Even if Imām al-Ḥujjah ﷻ wants to reappear, we—if only by our own sins—will oppose him for as long as we can!

In narrations, it has come that the scholars of Kūfah will write letters to Imām and advise him not to rise:

> We will take the responsibility to perform your obligations![46]

---

[45] Ibid., Vol. 1, p. 347.

[46] Ibid., Vol. 2, p. 253.

The Meaning of *Those Vested in Authority* (Ulī l-ʾamr)

﴿يَٰٓأَيُّهَا ٱلَّذِينَ ءَامَنُوٓاْ أَطِيعُواْ ٱللَّهَ وَأَطِيعُواْ ٱلرَّسُولَ وَأُوْلِي ٱلْأَمْرِ مِنكُمْۖ فَإِن تَنَٰزَعْتُمْ فِي شَيْءٖ فَرُدُّوهُ إِلَى ٱللَّهِ وَٱلرَّسُولِ إِن كُنتُمْ تُؤْمِنُونَ بِٱللَّهِ وَٱلْيَوْمِ ٱلْأٓخِرِۚ ذَٰلِكَ خَيْرٞ وَأَحْسَنُ تَأْوِيلًا﴾

﴿yā-ʾayyuhā lladhīna ʾāmanū ʾaṭīʿū llāha wa-ʾaṭīʿū r-rasūla wa-ʾulī l-ʾamri minkum fa-ʾin tanāzaʿtum fī shayʾin fa-ruddūhu ʾilā llāhi wa-r-rasūli ʾin kuntum tuʾminūna bi-llāhi wa-l-yawmi l-ʾākhiri dhālika khayrun wa-ʾaḥsanu taʾwīlaⁿ﴾

﴿O you who have faith! Obey Allah and obey the Apostle and those vested with authority among you. And if you dispute concerning anything, refer it to Allah and the Apostle, if you have faith in Allah and the Last Day. That is better and more favourable in outcome﴾[47]

Considering the narration,

أفضل الأعمال انتظار الفرج

The best of deeds is awaiting the relief (*Faraj*),

[47] Sūrat an-Nisāʾ, Verse 59.

which has also been verified in Sunnī sources, how could it be that the leadership of Islāmic countries should be for *those vested in authority (Ulī l-'amr)*?

If so, the faraj exists and is present! Why wait any longer for faraj?

With so much faraj, do we still want faraj? Then, what is the meaning of awaiting the faraj?[48]

Mischief At the End of Time

May God not let us walk astray from the path of the people of Truth and Ahl al-Bayt عليهم السلام, even if we must follow it within secrecy (taqiyyah). The taking away of belief from the believers is worse than them being put to death.

It has been said in narrations that the mischief *(fitnah)* that will afflict the believers

> is as dark as the layers of the night.

We see all this information and still wonder, if "The mischief will be as dark as the layers of the night" is true or not! Or whether the verses regarding the way of Ahl al-Bayt عليهم السلام are true or false (I seek refuge in God from this)! We still

[48] Ibid., Vol. 1, p. 61.

have doubts about all these happenings we see and foretold for us![49]

The Sweet Fruits of the Coming of Imām

This year, there is much coldness. May God make it a mercy and make the fruits of all the followers *(Shīʿah)* sweet with the reappearance of the Occulted One عجّل الله تعالى فرجه الشريف!

Usually, sweetness is something extra in addition to the usual and necessary, like a bonus, but Imām al-Mahdī's عجّل الله تعالى فرجه الشريف reappearance is of the highest vitality!

God knows what calamities that will befall the Muslims are worse during the occultation of that eminent one. During a short period, Germany managed to defeat 14 European countries. Greece was the biggest, which only took 25 days to overcome!

Having that in mind, the Islāmic countries are but a mouthpiece for them! But rapid advancement requires negligence of the enemy behind, where God has made all the powers of East and West a rival and torment to His enemies. And it is such that only the name of Islām will remain until the uprising of Imām al-Ḥujjah عجّل الله تعالى فرجه الشريف:

> From Islām, only its name will remain![50]

---

[49] *Mʿālim al-Huda*, p. 63.

[50] *Fī Riḥāb al-Shaykh Bahjat*, Vol. 2, p. 18.

Demolish And Rebuild!

In Riḍā Khān Pahlavī's time, they went to a person in Tehran and requested he visit Shaykh ʿAbd al-Karīm Hāʾrī ﷺ in Qom and, through unveiling/vision *(kashf),* receive the answer to the current obligation.

The person went and asked. On the first day, he (Āyatullāh Hāʾrī) said that the people must persist until they are killed!

But the second day, when the person again went to confirm the command given the day earlier, he said:

> It has nothing to do with me! This is a great calamity that will afflict the believers and Shīʿah that in the era of occultation, they are killed without being rescued. Accordingly, they must demolish and rebuild![51]

The Condition During the Occultation

Suppose two groups have faced each other and are in a state of war, and a person from one of these groups kidnaps the leader of the other group. That group has two alternatives: surrendering to their opponents or continuing the strife without a leader.

Now, we Muslims are almost in the same state as the infidels. The Muslims do not have a leader who can be

---

[51] Ibid., p. 298.

their flag bearer and spokesman, as the Sunnīs do not believe in Imāmate and Leadership at all, and the Shīʿah—despite believing in Imām عجل الله تعالى فرجه الشريف—in practice and obligations are just like the Sunnīs and do not differ from them.

Hence, now that the Muslims, whether Shīʿah or Sunnī, in belief or practice, do not have a leader, shouldn't they sit together and contemplate why?

Shouldn't we protect and defend ourselves? Shouldn't we gather and find how to protect our religion, faith, and worldly welfare from the enemies?

For example, one of the ways of protection and guard is firstly that we do not fall into the trap of the enemy; secondly, that we do not accept their gifts which they give to make us feel affection towards them and, through this, gain control over us Muslims and our interests and oppress us.

The closest of all heavenly religions to the Truth and reality are the Muslims, and from among the Muslims, those closest to Truth are the Shīʿah, who are seen as backward, low, downtrodden, and infidels.[52]

---

[52] Ibid., Vol. 1, p. 88.

The Trial of the Occultation

In past times, when the mausoleum of her eminence Lady Fāṭimah Maʿsūmah was crowded during Ziyārah and the women did not observe proper veiling (*hijāb*) Āyatullāh Burūjirdī said:

> It is not suitable for the people of knowledge to enter the mausoleum without urge among the heavy crowd. It is better if they are vigilant!

We hope that God will soon emerge as the Master for this handful of oppressed Shīʿahs, as in this world, there is no such record of a leader being absent from his army for such a long time.

What can be said? It is not known when! In all of the previous communities (*ummah*), the length of occultation has been prescribed, but in no community has such an occultation (as ours) occurred where no time has been set.

We Muslims have given our exams during the time of the Prophet and eleven Imāms in their presence! If this one also appeared, we would probably "come to his rescue" too!

Where were those who, during the Imāms, drawn towards Banū Umayyah and Banū al-ʿAbbās mad? Rather, among two ways, faith or the world *(dunya)*, chose the world opposite to the lasting abode! We have not seen the worldly sweetness, wealth, and abundance that they enjoyed; if we did, it is not certain if we would pass our exams (and instead become like them).

Mystical Climaxes During the Occultation

Everyone is not Salmān or ʾAbū Dharr, so they can endure the greatest calamities! Or like ʿAmmār, who was even ready to be killed!

The ranks they reached are closed. The entire world and all it contains are not worth one night's prayer of Salmān. May God have mercy on him. He sat on a cow skin and had an astonishing place for prayer!

Narratives have it that once they counted his household items, which were one skin, a bag of wheat, and a few other things, he still cried that his burden would be heavy tomorrow!

What rank did Salmān have? And what rank did his opposite, Muʿāwīya, have?

However, it has been said,

العبادة في زمن الغيبة أفضل من العبادة في زمن الحضور

> Worship during the occultation has more merit than worship during presence.

From this, one can understand that higher ranks are possible for us. If we lived during the time of the Messenger ﷺ and saw what ranks those around him possessed, such as Salmān, we would be incredibly encouraged to reach such high stations. But one who has not seen them is excused from not knowing about their states, and doubts will arise about whether he can also reach such ranks.

But we also have seen the spiritual powers of scholars, astounding and miraculous, which can not be described! And we were amazed at why others see and do not mention names! But we do not know why we are immovable in reaching such ranks![53]

---

[53] Ibid., p. 38.

The Duty of the Waiters

Imām al-Sajjad (Imām Zayn al-ʿĀbidīn) ﷺ said:

من ثبت على موالاتنا في غيبة قائمنا، أعطاه الله عزّ وجلّ أجر ألف شهيد من شهداء بدر وأحد

> Whoever remains steadfast in their loyalty to us during the occultation of our Qā'im, God ﷻ will grant them the reward of a thousand martyrs from the martyrs of Badr and Uḥud.[54]

The Prophet ﷺ said:

سلوا الله من فضله فإنّ الله عزّ وجلّ يحبّ أن يُسأل، وأفضل العبادة انتظار الفرج

> Ask God for His bounty, for God ﷻ loves to be asked, and the best act of worship is awaiting relief (al-Faraj).[55]

Duties During the Era of Occultation

May God guide and help us to find the way to open and expand our hearts and minds so that we, with their help, may liberate ourselves from the chain of inner ignorance and doubt.

---

[54] *Muʿjam Aḥadīth al-Imām al-Mahdī* ﷺ, Vol. 3, p. 197.

[55] Ibid., Vol. 1, p. 248.

The reappearance, even if only for an hour, will bring enlightenment afterward. Enlightenment is also faraj.

Have we thought of a way to reach this event?

At times our Imāms عليهم السلام has made this the completion of the proof (*iṭmi'nān al-Ḥujjah*) upon us, and hence have said:

> Pray ardently for the reappearance.

However, not just by mere utterance with the tongue!

They have also said that we should behave like the initial acts of behavior. In other words, we should behave in new situations as we have acted in the past.

Our Imāms عليهم السلام have taught us to act with certitude, and in cases when we do not have certitude, we should halt and act with precaution.[56]

The Office of the Imām of the Age عجل الله تعالى فرجه الشريف

God knows what sort of person we are counted as in the notebook of the Imām of Time عجل الله تعالى فرجه الشريف, a person who is told the servants' deeds twice a week (Monday and Thursday)! All we know is that the way we should be, we are not.[57]

---

[56] *Fī Riḥāb al-Shaykh Bahjat*, Vol. 1, p. 23.

[57] Ibid., Vol. 2, p. 120.

Preparedness For the Appearance

If the Imām's awaited return, peace be upon him, is close, then every person should prepare himself that day.

An example of one of the ways to prepare is to make repentance. This repentance will ward off all the calamities which have befallen the Shīʿahs, which are without likeness, and other calamities which will come before the reappearance of Imām.[58]

Are We Truly Waiters?

For a thousand years, our Imāms reported that the calamities that will afflict the people of faith will be so severe that many will lose their faith! Does walking away from faith result in walking away from calamities?

Are we truly among the waiters of the Imām of Time?

Do we also want the Imām of Time to reappear? Are we satisfied with his reappearance?

Is that eminent one pleased with our actions?

Is the Imām pleased that we are spending his resources and property in an unfitting way as if it is not even his property?

---

[58] Ibid., p. 109.

Is the Imām ﷼ pleased with our neglectfulness regarding following his and his father's path, opinions, commands, and love? Peace be upon them. Or that we entirely abandon it?

Believing in the Imām

Doubts in the existence of the Imām of the Age ﷼ and opposition to him come from a group of people who lack belief in the Imāmate of his eminent father, Imām Ḥasan b. ʿAlī al-ʿAskarī ﷼. Those who have faith in the Imāmate of Imām Ḥasan al-ʿAskarī ﷼ also believe in his successor, his beloved son Mahdī ﷼, and his being alive until his reappearance.

Famous narrations quoted from his eminent father and his testament to his successor and beloved son are definite documents, and there are no doubts about their validity.

Also, his existence and life are religious requirements; hence, all Muslims believe in long lives for certain individuals.

Moreover, the visions of the righteous, the general scholars, and others, and the encounters with the Imām from those who have been healed and sought help in the East and West are of such huge numbers that one finds them truthfully. And I will guarantee such certitude!

I will make another point to what has already been said, namely that in the tradition of two weighty things (*Ḥadīth al-Thaqalayn*), which is authentic (*mutawātir*) among both Sunnī and Shīʿah, it has been reported from the great Prophet of Islām ﷺ that the Qurʾān, the Imām, and the Progeny will not be separated from each other until Judgement Day.

The conclusion is that in every era, one has the Qurʾān; one must also have an Imām alongside it, and faith in one is equivalent to faith in the other.[59]

Faith in the Imām!

Man afflicts himself with what even his enemy does not do to him! Namely to dry and wipe out the source of prosperity and peace! Consequently, it is not certain if everyone will have true inner faith and conviction in the Imām عجل الله تعالى فرجه الشريف at the time of his reappearance. Some profess faith only out of constraint!

Perfect Belief!

Suppose we are in a room with a shut door and know that big powers, such as the USA or the former Soviet Union, are standing behind the door, listening to our talk for or against them, recording it, and later using it against us. In that case, we will become so frightened and careful what we

---

59 *Naḥwa al-Ḥabīb*, p. 60.

say! Even though we cannot see them, we know they are behind the door.

Then why do we not behave like this when it comes to the Imām of Time ﻋﺠﻞ ﺍﻟﻠﻪ ﺗﻌﺎﻟﻰ ﻓﺮﺟﻪ ﺍﻟﺸﺮﻳﻒ, acting for or against issues concerned with him? And no difference between us and Ahl al-Sunnah do not have such a belief?

Complete Presence of the Imām

Some think the Imāms ﻋﻠﻴﻬﻢ ﺍﻟﺴﻼﻡ do not hear or are just like ordinary men. One of the Sunnī school followers passed the holy cellar of Sāmarrā' (*sirdar Samara*) and heard a person inside the cellar repeatedly say,

> O Master of Time!

That passer-by said mockingly,

> O Master of Time! O Master of Time! Say so much until he answers you!

They do not understand! They are entirely unreasonable! The Imāms ﻋﻠﻴﻬﻢ ﺍﻟﺴﻼﻡ is the all-seeing eye and all-hearing, all-hearing ear of God, who, if something is uttered, knows and hears it even before all those in the gathering hear it!

Complete Following

The one who has faith in and conviction of the Creator and the creation, has belief in and a bond with the Prophets and their successors ﷺ, turns to them (*tawassul*)[60] in his belief and deeds, walks and halts according to their commands, in worship empties his heart from all other than God and wholeheartedly performs the prayer (which everything depends upon), in doubtful situations follows the Imām of the Age ﷺ—in other words distances himself from all that which is against the Imām and approaches everything which is with the Imām, curse the one whom the Imām curses and is compassionate towards the one whom the Imām is compassionate to—a person who possesses all these characteristics and attributes will not lack any perfection and will not have any trouble.

---

[60] The term *tawassul* is often translated as "intercession," but this does not fully capture its meaning in this context. In Islāmic theology, tawassul refers to seeking nearness to God ﷻ through an intermediary, such as a prophet or a saint, by asking them to pray on one's behalf or act as a means (*wasīla*) of divine assistance. It involves turning to these intermediaries with faith in their closeness to God ﷻ and the ability to intercede while firmly believing that all help ultimately comes from God ﷻ.

In this context, tawassul describes turning to the Prophets and their successors with faith, belief, and deeds, seeking their guidance and connection to God ﷻ. Depending on the text's purpose, tawassul can be rendered as "seeking means," 'turning to," or "besought" while retaining its devotional undertone.

Perfect Nobility of the Imām of the Age عجل الله تعالى فرجه الشريف

The Imām of Time عجل الله تعالى فرجه الشريف has complete control during the occultation era and is the first saying in all affairs; hence, it is also active.

He sent a multitude of letters and orders to Mīrzā Bozorg Shīrāzī.

For example, once a person brought an order to Mīrzā, who took it, read it, and gave a small amount of money, perhaps two dinars today, to the person who left.

Another person there saw that at the end of the order was the stamp and signature of the Imām of Time عجل الله تعالى فرجه الشريف! He asked,

> Is the order from the Imām of the Age?

Mīrzā answered,

> Yes!

The person said,

> Then why did you give so little money considering that the master sent the order, and hence you should be more generous?

Mīrzā said,

You have only seen this one order from him and not all the others![61]

The Ways of Communion

The ways to communion with God is through obedience to God and the Imām of Time عجل الله تعالى فرجه الشريف, and the criteria for this is by acting according to the notebook of Sharīʿa, that is, *al-Risālah al-ʿAmaliyyah al-Ṣaḥīḥah*.[62]

A Strong Bond With the Imām

We must know that our remedy lies in self-building in all aspects; without this, we are incapable, and our work will not end.

Admitting that actions come from ourselves, which we have thought and think of; if we do not improve ourselves and establish a bond with God and His representatives, our task will not be accomplished; neither today, tomorrow, nor the day after tomorrow—what accomplishment is this?

Will our conduct be correct if we do not establish a strong bond with the Master of Command, Imām of Time عجل الله تعالى فرجه الشريف, and build our Selves?

---

[61] During a lesson in Khārij al-Fiqh (Wednesday 9-8-1382 (2003)).

[62] *Naḥwa al-Ḥabīb*, p. 62.

As we are now, will our task truly be accomplished if we do not improve our conduct?[63]

The Way To Establishment, Love, And Communion

The way to establish a bond with Ahl al-Bayt (a) and particularly his eminence, the Patron of the Age (aj), consists of:

1. Knowledge and insight of the Almighty God

2. Complete obedience to God

These two will develop a love for God and towards all those whom God loves, such as the Prophets and the Apostles, and it will especially create an attachment and bond to Muḥammad (s) and his family (a), among whom the Master of Time (aj) is closest to us.[64]

A Seeing Eye And A Hearing Ear

Something that will embarrass and shame us is that Imām knows and hears all things; they are God's seeing eye and hearing ear.

---

[63] Ibid., p. 104.

[64] Ibid., p. 61.

What have we done to achieve proximity and closeness to them? You are seekers of presence and reappearance, so why don't you do something so you always see yourselves beside that Master? He sees us, and we do not see him! Then why are we so far away?[65]

Closeness To the Master of Time عجل الله تعالى فرجه الشريف

In our solitude with God, in our invocations, repentance, prayers, and worship, we should read especially the noble invocation of *Du‘ā’ ‘Aẓumal-Bala*’[66] and want from God that he sends the Master of Time عجل الله تعالى فرجه الشريف!

We should be with him and, whether he now comes or not, do not walk away from him or his satisfaction. He sees, and he knows what we say to each other!

He is God's seeing eye and hearing ear, and he hears our words before ourselves! When we utter a word, the sound comes from our mouths toward our ears; there is a distance between the mouth and the ear, and He precedes this distance and hears what we say before we hear it! Considering this, can we do something without him being aware? Can we do something without him knowing?[67]

---

[65] *Mā Warā’ al-Sukūt*, p. 228.

[66] His Eminence highly recommended frequent recitation of this Du‘ā’, which we have added in full to the end of this book.

[67] *Naḥwa al-Ḥabīb*, p. 109.

Maintaining Communion With the Imām

If we know that we are in the presence of *Ein Allāh an-Nadhira,* God's seeing eye, do we have the nerve to ask for an encounter with the Occulted One, bearing in mind that we act opposite to his satisfaction?

We let go of prayers and fasting and replace them with backbiting and slander!

Do we want him to tell us,

> I have made the forbidden lawful for you and removed the obligations from you?

What is meant is that what would have happened if we maintained our bond with that Master through divine servitude?

Others did not let us, even if we are also to be blamed for not wanting the bond between us and Imām to be maintained. Otherwise, every person would find, have a bond, and a conviction, and (consequently) a day would come when each person would improve himself, become his follower, and have a happy ending.

Necessaries of the Waiting

Mere waiting for the reappearance is not enough! Support, or rather obedience and servitude, are also required. This is especially significant considering what events will happen before the Imām of Time emerges, to such extent that the saying "the Earth will be filled with injustice" will become realized. God knows what afflicts persons through their lack of faith! May God make the emergence of that master prosperity to the fullest extent for the people of faith and hasten his reappearance.

Is it possible that absolute prosperity comes about without faith, obedience, and servitude? May God grant success to the people of faith from being led astray.

The Method of Concealing One's Faith (*Taqiyyah*)[68]

The Shīʿah Imāmiyyah school of thought has stayed alive through concealing one's faith (taqiyyah). Considering this, is it correct not to recognize concealing faith as a part of the religion and separate it from religion?

They asked Ḥusayn b. Ruḥ about the successor of the Prophet in a public gathering where both Shīʿah and Sunnī were present. In reply, he said,

> In our opinion, it is correct that Abū Bakr was the caliph after the Messenger of God!

---

68 Taqiyyah means precautionary dissimulation or denial of religious belief and practice in the face of persecution.

After this, the Sunnīs said,

> Until when will they lie about this Shaykh?

The Imām elected representative practiced concealing the faith (taqiyyah).

Similarly, after the uprising of Imām Ḥusayn, no other of the Imāms thought of uprising to such a degree that Imām ʿAlī al-Hādī and Imām Ḥasan al-ʿAskarī were even prisoned (without uprising).

Requirement of the Waiting!

The Qurʾān is a book filled with light and guidance towards the Imām. The proof of God (ḥujjah) may be among the people or us without the Imām. What is within our reach is to act to bring about the reappearance.

Waiting for the Imām of Time's reappearance is incompatible with hurting his friends. For years now, the friends of that Master from both parts of this war have been killed, which draws sorrow upon him, but outwardly, his hands are tied, and he cannot do a thing!

But how loving and kind Master is toward those who mention his name, call upon him, and turn to him for help! He is more loving towards them than their fathers.

If we fall into negligence, do not pray and supplicate, and shut our eyes to all these calamities, we must either not count them as Muslims or ourselves! And if we are not merciful towards them, no one will be merciful towards us.[69]

The Friend of the Prince

We love the Imām of Time ﷺ because he is the bee prince; our affairs reach us completely through him, and the Prophet ﷺ has appointed him as our leader.

We love the Prophet ﷺ because God has made him the bond between us and Himself. We love God because He is the source of all blessings, and it is from His bounties that all potentialities come into existence.

Hence, if we want ourselves and our perfections, we must be God's friend, and if we are God's friend, we must be the friends of His blessed bonds, the Prophet ﷺ and his successor. Otherwise, we are not friends with ourselves, the Generous Giver (God), or the Link of Blessings (the Prophet ﷺ and the Imāms ﷺ).

The Consent of the Imām of the Age ﷺ

If we act upon those articles of faith which there is no doubt regarding, we will realize in our sleep and when

[69] *Fī Riḥāb al-Shaykh Bahjat*, Vol. 2, p. 366.

giving account which of our deeds definitely pleases the Imām of Time عجل الله تعالى فرجه الشريف and which ones sadden him.

A person who acts according to certain commands of the religion and, at times of doubts regarding the following of a creating religious leader (*taqlīd*), acts with caution will not feel regret even if, for example, it later turns out that the person's religious leader did not fulfill the criterion to be followed. This is so since such a person (through his caution) has acted according to all religious leaders' directions and all religious verdicts.

Achieving the Satisfaction of the Imām of the Age عجل الله تعالى فرجه الشريف

In social affairs, we should not look upon others and follow this one or that one as they are not infallible, no matter how great or noble they are! Rather, we must see if we would act in such a way if we were alone and no one was present.

We should not look upon others. We should not compare ourselves with Ahl al-Sunnah. Rather, we must achieve the satisfaction of the Imām of Time عجل الله تعالى فرجه الشريف in our actions, in spending part of the Imām عجل الله تعالى فرجه الشريف (in khums), as well as in other social affairs.[70]

[70] Ibid., Vol. 1, p. 101.

In the Way of the Imām

Some animals, such as the honeybee or animals that give milk, are profitable for people. Man can also be profitable for religion and people.

Accordingly, if we work to our best efforts to guide the people, is it possible that we will not have the favor of "God's watchful eye," the Imām of Time عجّل الله تعالى فرجه الشريف?

If we are in the way of Imām, we should not be sad no matter how badly they speak of us or mock us. Rather, we should proceed on that path of Truth with firm steps and endure the difficulties we may face.[71]

The Dissatisfaction of the Imām of Time عجّل الله تعالى فرجه الشريف

Woe upon the one about whom Imām al-Ḥujjah عجّل الله تعالى فرجه الشريف knows that he is indifferent and nonchalant when it comes to achieving the Imām's satisfaction or distancing himself from that which the Imām disapproves.

In material affairs, he tells the people his hand is the Imām's, and he is the Imām's representative, which is not the case in other affairs!

God save us from being like that! Especially considering that we want that at the end of our life and deathbed, he

---

[71] Ibid., p. 103.

comes to our rescue, and through his intercession, our calamities may be lifted. Is it possible that we are distant from him at the beginning and then at the end have the inclination for his help?

A doctor near his death greeted all the illuminated infallible عليهم السلام and paid homage to them, but no one among those present saw any person!

We should not act in a way so those great ones which we need tell us at our last breath,

> We do not know this person!

The difference in rank of faith, piety (taqwa), and certitude between us and past scholars is huge! A hundred years span between us and them is like a thousand years! They prayed and were answered fast; it was something usual for them. But nowadays, it is very rare that someone says,

> I prayed, and my prayer was answered.

It has been narrated that a person whose death lasted a week with Shaykh ʿAbd al-Karīm Hā'irī قدس سره was in Mashhad, and his family was in ʿIrāq. He visited the mausoleum of Imām ʿAlī ar-Riḍā عليه السلام and said,

> My family!

Without delay, a person passed by him and gave him some money, but he turned towards Imām عليه السلام and said,

This is not in measure with your generosity!

Another amount reached him, but he said again,

It is too little!

After this, one from among the scholars of Mashhad, who was present, approached him and said,

It is apparent that your trade with Imām is good!

He then stretched into his pocket and gave the same amount of money that the person desired.[72]

Neglecting the Present Imām

Every person must think upon himself and find a way to develop a bond with Imām al-Ḥujjah عجل الله تعالى فرجه الشريف and relieve himself whether that Master's reappearance is close!

There has been a group for whom the Occulted One عجل الله تعالى فرجه الشريف has been present and apparent at times as if they have connected to him without any wire and have answered on his behalf!

Muqaddas Ardabīlī قدس سره and Sayyid Baḥr al-ʿUlūm قدس سره, about whom the probability of lies coming from them is none, did not approve of the expression *fa ʿalayhī lʿanat Allāh* which means "may the curse of God upon him." They said

[72] Ibid., p. 101.

that such expressions are associated with *Bahā'iyyah* and those who falsely claim to be al-Mahdī.

Developing a bond, connecting to Imām, and bringing about personal faraj is an affair concerned with ourselves contrary to general faraj. Thus, why don't we pay attention to establishing a bond with that Master and neglect such a thing? And at the same time, we focus on the general reappearance and encounter with Imām! If we do not commit ourselves to personal relief through self-building, there is a fear that at the time of reappearance, we will flee from that Master!

Because our path is one for those who do not pay attention to important matters.

The sun's task is to shine no matter how thick and many the clouds are. The Master of Time ﷽ is also like this, no matter how thick the veil of occultation is!

Our Holy Prophet ﷺ has said (regarding most of us) that our eyes do not see, but there is and has been a handful who sees, and if they do not see, they have a bond with the Imām ﷽!

A person from the Zaydi school of thought said,

> Every Imām whose body is not seen has not the worth of even a grain!

In reply, a Sunnī person said,

> 12 Imāmi Shīʿah say that the Imām is occulted, but you, who also are Zaydi, say that an Imām who cannot be seen has not even the worth of a grain. Hence, it is apparent that you are on the wrong side!

We have seen persons who seem to have communication with Imām; whatever they said or wanted happened!

One person in the desert said three times,

> O Imām of Time! Send me a vehicle!

Instantly, a vehicle appeared that he could travel with.

Yes, that Master is so close to us and aware of our state, but we who do not see him neglect him and imagine we are far away!

It is a pity that we do not grasp the blessing of guardianship (*wilāyah*)![73]

It Is Not Required That the Imām Comes!

Anyhow—for the hasten of reappearance, lifting of affliction and calamities, rescue and improvement of the believers' state—we must say,

---

[73] Ibid., Vol. 2, pp. 133–135.

> O God! Put an end to the sufferings of the people, through his reappearance.

As oppression, tyranny, calamities, and pressure have truly befallen Islām and the Muslims, especially the people of faith, the knife has reached the bone.

Not once or twice, but many times, have I heard some persons say,

> When others were leaders and sources of emulation (marājiʿ), Imām did not come; now that the leadership and guidance have reached us, he is going to appear?

The talks of these persons are like the talks of some persons who, according to narrations, at the time of reappearance, write a letter to the Occulted One عجل الله تعالى فرجه الشريف saying,

> We are responsible for all the work and efforts you do not need for you to come and intervene!

Oppressing the Imām

What a marvelous thing the Qur'ān is, telling us about what can be seen and heard at all the different times of revelation.

The peer of the Qur'ān (Ahl al-Bayt عليهم السلام) also tells us about the world's blessings. But we do not know the worth of our sympathizers, guides, defenders, and patrons but instead kill them just like the community of Prophet Ṣāliḥ ﷺ who killed the sent camel, which was a source of blessings for them.

We cannot see our Imāms ﷺ, the custodians of our blessings and the bond between us and God.

If the Imām of Time ﷺ comes, we will make the same deal with him as his pure forefathers! Is it possible that the Imām of Time ﷺ has 400 million followers and does not reappear?[74]

We Have Tied the Hands of Imām!

What should we do to our inner and outer problems? What have we done so we are afflicted with these problems? We must ponder what we have done so we are left without any guardian.

The problem is that we have not and will not build ourselves! We are not ready to build ourselves!

The noble Prophet ﷺ said,

> Are you not aware of your pain and cure? Your pain is sin, and your cure is repentance.

---

[74] Ibid., Vol. 1, p. 12.

We want to do whatever we desire, but others cannot hurt us. We do whatever we want towards our dear ones and friends, but others, the enemies, are not allowed to hurt us!

If we build ourselves, God is enough; God is the guide. But we do not want to build ourselves, and we do not want to be pained by others.

The evil ones will continue doing their deeds unless an appropriate and sufficient patron stops them.

If we were on the path, we would walk it. Who killed the Commander of the Faithful (Amīr al-Mu'minīn عليه السلام)? Who killed Ḥusayn b. 'Alī عليه السلام?

Who has tied the one who is now (Imām of Time عجل الله تعالى فرجه الشريف) for a thousand years?

We are not prepared to build ourselves. If we build ourselves slowly, humanity will be built entirely.[75]

The Watching Eye of God

Is it possible that a person works for the guidance of people to the best of his efforts and be like Imām Mahdī عجل الله تعالى فرجه الشريف and then does not have the favor of the watchful eye of God?

---

[75] *Naḥwa al-Ḥabīb*, p. 101-102.

Woe upon the state of a person who considers the assistance of oppression or defending oppression to be good!

Oh, if we only realized this world's emptiness and nothingness, did not give much value to anything, and did not dispute and quarrel so much over nothing!

Shooting the Imām!

May God have mercy upon Kūhestānī ؒ.[76] The custom he laid in (the province of) Māzandarān (Irān) can not be found elsewhere. Even though the cities of Māzandarān lay close to each other, he built a religious school (*Madrassah*) for the religious students in every city.

One of the fellow students said,

> During Muḥammad Riḍā Pahlavī's time, they came on behalf of the regime to give him some money, but he did not accept.

He also did not accept money from Ḥajj Burūjirdī and said,

[76] He was born in 1303 A.H (1884 A.D) in Kūhsān (famous as *Kūhistān* today). He finished his primary education in Būshahr and moved to Najaf in 1340 A.H (1921 A.D). After staying 10 years in Najaf, he returned to Kūhistān. He left this world in 1392 A.H (1973 A.D) at 84. He spent his life in asceticism, piety (taqwa), and self-building. His encounters with the Patron of the Age, may our souls be sacrificed for him, are well known.

> If I accept this, I can not continue to advise the scholars ('Ulamā') that I am giving currently!

May God grant us the success not to shoot arrows at Imām عجل الله تعالى فرجه الشريف![77]

The Signature of Imām of Time عجل الله تعالى فرجه الشريف

We students must consider how we can receive the support and signature of our Master, the Patron of the Age عجل الله تعالى فرجه الشريف. That is, how we should study and act so our Master assists us and signs our deeds.

A student's thoughts, focus, and sorrow should always be on how he should behave, act, and talk so that his Master approves of him, whether during his studies or after.

If a student always is in these thoughts and walks on this path on how to receive the signature of approval from his Master, he will not be led astray—neither in his works, talks, or behavior.

Neither will he act in contradiction with his Master. Such a disciple will never walk astray or feel regret.

---

[77] *Fī Riḥāb al-Shaykh Bahjat*, Vol. 1, p. 253.

Present Among the Mystics

We want from God, with the Prophets ﷺ, the successors عليهم السلام, and the current Apostle عجّل الله تعالى فرجه الشريف, who is present among the mystics, as an intermediate, that we do not deviate from being godly, be with the godly and God's intermediates. He makes us see and know ourselves and the godly ones. Then, their opposites will also be known.[78]

The Effects From Duʿāʾ al-Faraj

If Duʿāʾ al-Faraj does not bring about general faraj, it will at least bring relief to the supplicating one, God-willing.

Just as it has been narrated in some traditions,

> Pray, for in it lays your faraj.[79]

The Sorrows of the Imām of the Age عجّل الله تعالى فرجه الشريف

Now that a handful of Shīʿah—among those scholars-women and children, who neither have any sanctuary nor any refuge, are afflicted with problems, shouldn't we pray to God with a weeping eye and a broken heart that He lifts the calamities?

---

[78] *Mā Warāʾ al-Ṣamt*, p. 81.

[79] *ʿĀlam al-Ghayb*, p. 55.

Is it right that we sit comfortably and watch while our brothers and sisters in faith are in difficulties due to oppressors?

We will face similar calamities if we do not sympathize with them and pray for their rescue today and tomorrow. Others will not pray or show sympathy for us, either.

Should our leader and Master, the Patron of the Age ﷺ, be in sorrow, and we are happy?

We should be laughing and joyful while he cries at what effects calamities leave upon his friends.

At the same time, we consider ourselves his followers?[80]

Shelter For the Believers

If the people of faith come to know their real shelter—that is, the Master of Time ﷺ—and seek refuge with him, is it then possible in this aspect that his favor upon them may not be realized?[81]

Ardent Attentiveness And Turning (To Him)

The Book and the Progeny ﷺ have reached us through inheritance; we must use them more than others.

---

[80] *Fī Riḥāb al-Shaykh Bahjat*, Vol. 2, p. 181.

[81] Ibid., p. 254.

Some people turned to Shaykh Ḥasan ʿAlī Tihrānī as an intermediate and also saw the effects of this intercession, but they were not aware of the Imām of the Age!

We must turn to the Imām more than these persons to see the effects. Certainly, the Imām of the Age leaves better effects than anyone else.[82]

Fearful Heart in Prayer

To have a fearful heart during prayer, truly turning (*tawassul*) to the Imām of Time prior to the prayer will make you perform the prayer with absolute completeness.[83]

The Perfection of Man

The perfection of man lies in servitude, and servitude is the abandonment of sin in belief and deeds.

The perfect person is the guide, the Patron of the Age in this era. The path to receiving his guidance is to continuously, with sincerity and honesty, and without doubt, perform known supplications (tawassul), such as Ziyārat Maʾthūrah[84], and the prayers of the Imām.

---

[82] *ʿĀlam al-Ghayb*, p. 55.

[83] *Naḥwa al-Ḥabīb*, p. 63.

[84] The phrase Ziyārat Maʾthūrah refers to a transmitted supplicatory visitation (ziyārah)—meaning a ziyārah text that has been narrated from the Prophet or the Imāms.

Peace and salutations be upon God and all His friends!

Public Invocations

There are many problems and calamities that the Shīʿah are afflicted with today, including diverse diseases, cancer, and accidents; hence, we must humbly pray and supplicate at holy places to end all these misfortunes.

Āyatullāh Khumaynī (q) said,

> Sayyid ʿAbd al-Hādī Shīrāzī came to Irān for medical treatment and then went to the holy city of Mashhad. I went to see him. He had lost his eyesight and asked all those around him to pray for him.

The misfortunes and calamities which the Shīʿah are troubled with today are considerably more than those which Sayyid ʿAbd al-Hādī had to endure. We must wish all too deeply to pray, beg, and supplicate so that perhaps the door of relief is opened.

Reforming the Self Is the Symbol of Communion

We must know that self-building is our cure in all aspects, without which we will be incapable, and our problems will be endless. We must admit that as long as we do not reform ourselves and do not get in touch with God and His representatives, our problems will not be solved, nor will they be solved if we postpone them until tomorrow or the day after.

Until we do not have a strong bond with the Imām of Time عجل الله تعالى فرجه الشريف, our problems will not be solved. And the strength of our bond with the Patron of the Age عجل الله تعالى فرجه الشريف also lies in self-building.[85]

Continuous Presence

We must act as if the Imām of Time عجل الله تعالى فرجه الشريف is present. Where he goes, we should go; what he does, we should do, and what he abandons, we must abandon!

And if we do not know, we can at least act upon precaution!

But sometimes we do not want to be on the path of that Master's satisfaction, not that we do not know what his satisfaction lies in or cannot reach it.[86]

The Veils of Seeing

Where did those go with a tie with the Imām of Time عجل الله تعالى فرجه الشريف? We have rendered ourselves helpless and sometimes do not have a thing by cutting relations with him! Were they poorer than us?

---

[85] *'Ālam al-Ghayb*, p. 65.

[86] *Fī Riḥāb al-Shaykh Bahjat*, Vol. 2, p. 386.

If you say: our hands do not reach that Master! You answer why were you not hard upon yourselves in performing the obligatory and abandoning the forbidden?

He is satisfied with us:

> The most virtuous of people abstain from the forbidden.

Abandoning the obligatory and committing the forbidden are the veils and curtains covering our sight from that master.[87]

The Most Vital Invocation With Outcome

The most vital invocation is Imām al-Mahdī's Du'ā' al-Faraj. All the problems of the people and the governments stream from the occultation of that Master. We must pray for the lifting of social calamities and the fulfillment of people's wishes to the same extent that we pray for solving our difficulties.

Sayyid Ibn Ṭāwūs went to the holy mausoleum of Amīr al-Mu'minīn, cursed the local judge, and then said,

> It will cause your destruction in three days!

And that is what happened.

---

[87] Ibid., Vol. 1, p. 361.

Sayyid Ibn Ṭāwūs stated in the book *Iqbāl* that he has divine inspiration (*'ilhām*) and mentioned some examples. He was among those regarding whom it has been said that he did not since once in his entire life![88]

Praying For Imām

The Occulted One ﷻ has the most extensive knowledge and possesses the Greatest Name of God. He has told many who have seen him in dreams or awake to pray for him!

Even though he can bring the dead to life, he himself is jailed in a big prison. He gives special attentiveness to others, especially in individual affairs. But when it comes to social affairs concerning the Imām himself, he has no right to do so!

May God strengthen the bond between the Imām of Time ﷻ, the Shī'ah, and people of faith so that we may be patient and endure when patience is needed.

This narration is reported from the Sunnīs, where the eminent Messenger ﷺ said,

أفضل أعمال أمّتي انتظار الفرج

---

[88] *'Ālam al-Ghayb*, p. 363.

> The best of deeds for my nation (Ummah) is awaiting the relief (Faraj).[89]

Du'ā' al-Faraj—the Invocation For Humanity

If a person prays from the bottom of his heart for believing men and women while he does not pray for himself, the angels will pray for him instead.

If someone prays for himself, it is possible that his prayer may not be granted due to not fulfilling the conditions of invocation or some other obstacle. But when angels pray, there are no obstacles or lack of attention, and their prayers are surely heard.

Prayers for the people of faith and those who are counted as people of faith are prayers for the Great Leader, the absolute guardian and savior of this time. And prayers for him are prayers for the entire humanity.[90]

Du'ā' al-Faraj—the Invocation For Afflictions

The prayer for hastening the faraj is our prayer of greetings.

In narrations, it has come that everyone will be ruined at the end of time except those who pray for faraj.

---

[89] *Fī Riḥāb al-Shaykh Bahjat*, Vol. 2, p. 299.

[90] *Mā Warā' al-Ṣamt*, p. 83.

With these words, our Imāms ﷺ have granted much favor to the people of faith and the Shīʿah so they may come to know themselves. It is a sign for them; praying for faraj is a sign of one's faith still being firm.

They have also given other remarkable commands, as at the end of time, the difficulties for the people of faith will be very hard to such extent that it is said,

> ...after which the Earth will be filled with injustice and oppression.

Possibly, it also comes in narrations that

> most of those who believe in the leadership (Imāmate) of that master will deny him.

They have also commanded that at the end of time, we should read this invocation of faraj, which is an invocation to stay firm in our religion:

يا الله يا رحمان يا رحيم، يا مقلب القلوب، ثبت قلبي على دينك

> *O God, O the Beneficent, O the Merciful, O Turner of hearts, make my heart steadfast upon Your religion*[91]

---

[91] Majlisī, ʿAllamah Muḥammad Bāqir, *Biḥār al-Anwār*, Vol. 52, p. 148.

In other words, preserve that degree of faith that You have granted me—not being a Muslim and being kept as a Muslim because that is not firmness in religion.

These turnings for intercession (tawassul), mourning ceremonies, and visiting the graves of Ahl al-Bayt ﷺ (Ziyārah) are a sign that the people of faith are connected and close to them and have not yet walked astray from them. That is why the infidels and their servants wanted to separate Muslims from the Qur'ān, let alone mosques and mourning ceremonies, as these were all against the desires of the tyrannical powers. Consequently, they commanded the ruining of graves and shutting down of mourning ceremonies as well.

The 8th of the month of Shawwāl, which is the day the graves of the Imāms of Bāqī ﷺ were demolished, was, as per custom, a day off in the Islāmic seminary in Najaf, but we slowly became used to it, and eventually, it was something normal for us![92]

Relief From Calamities Through Duʿāʾ al-Faraj

In difficulties and calamities, Duʿāʾ al-Faraj must be read a great deal as Duʿāʾ al-Faraj is the invocation of personal faraj! That is why, during severe times, one must be attached to that invocation.

---

[92] *Fī Riḥāb al-Shaykh Bahjat*, Vol. 1, p. 363.

When they were going to whip the son of Ḥasan b. ʿAlī 🕮, the son-in-law of Ḥusayn b. ʿAlī 🕮, 500 times according to the order of Walīd, Imām al-Sajjad (Imām Zayn al-ʿĀbidīn) 🕮 told him,

My cousin! Do not forget Duʿāʾ al-Faraj!

He replied,

My cousin! What is Duʿāʾ al-Faraj?

Imām al-Sajjad 🕮 taught him the prayer, whereupon the son of Ḥasan b. ʿAlī 🕮 started reciting it.

Someone who was appointed as his assassin stepped down from the pulpit and said,

I see (in him) a person who has endured much oppression! I will postpone his death until I have spoken with the leader (Walīd).

And it was postponed until Walid was consulted, who ordered that he should be released.[93]

Certain Outcomes From Duʿāʾ al-Faraj

The Muslims are weak in the hands of the infidels, and the infidels have power and authority over the Muslims through the Muslims' wealth and resources!

---

[93] *Al-Tahdhīb*, Vol. 3, p. 294.

Isn't it negligence and conceit on our behalf to live happily (ignoring) all this contempt and oppression (directed at us)?

How should bloodthirsty wolves attack a group of sheep with no guardian, leader, or shepherd from all sides?

God knows how the infidels sit and draw schemes on how to render the Islāmic countries weak, low, and enslaved!

How much we must think upon the Occulted One عجل الله تعالى فرجه الشريف and pray for the hastening of his reappearance! Devoted invocations for the hastening of reappearance have an effect, but not mere tongue movements, like dryly and emptily saying "hasten the reappearance!" at the end of sermons to make the people rise!

Duʿāʾ for the hastening of faraj is like supererogatory prayer, a recommended deed. That is, we truly and sincerely, with sorrow, should want from God that the span of a thousand and some years which has fallen between the people and the divine link comes to an end.

No prayers and supplications are performed in a state of sorrow, sadness, and inner engagement by people; if they had been, the situation would not be as it is. The reappearance is at a certain and chosen time; the Imām عجل الله تعالى فرجه الشريف will come at that time.

Du'ā' al-Faraj

The best deed to not be ruined at the end of time is the Faraj of the Imām of Time عجل الله تعالى فرجه الشريف. of course, a Du'ā' al-Faraj leaves an effect on all our actions![94]

Invocation During the Pilgrimage

When you go for the pilgrimage (Ḥajj), you want from God the most important of wishes, that is, the coming of his eminence, the Master of the Age عجل الله تعالى فرجه الشريف, which also is the faraj of humanity. And after that, pray for the removal of corrupt and tyrannical regimes.[95]

Conditions And Results of Du'ā' al-Faraj

What calamities befall the Imām of Time عجل الله تعالى فرجه الشريف, the king of the entire Earth and around whom all affairs circulate? In what state is that Master, and in what state are we? While he is in prison and has no comfort or joy, we are negligent and unmindful of this!

Those who have had the honor to meet that Master in dreams or awake have heard that he has said,

> Pray ardently for my coming (Faraj).

---

[94] *M'ālim al-Huda*, p. 72.

[95] *'Ālam al-Ghayb*, p. 53.

God knows how many these prayers must be so that the reappearance will be appropriate! If some are serious and sincere in their invocations and share the joy and grief of Ahl al-Bayt, they will undoubtedly have visions and certainly not be blind like us.

Invocations must be performed by observing the conditions. Repentance, among other things, is one condition for a proper invocation, according to the saying,

> The prayer of one who has repented is granted.

We should not act in a way that we pray for the hastening of reappearance and, at the same time, act in a way that postpones the coming of that Master![96]

True Invocation

Those who are truthful in their invocations are happy at the joy and sad at the sorrow of Ahl al-Bayt see things and have visions; without any doubt, they have, and indeed, they are not blindfolded as us.

God forbid that we pray for the hastening of the Imām of Time's reappearance while our actions postpone his coming![97]

---

[96] *Fī Riḥāb al-Shaykh Bahjat*, Vol. 1, p. 118.

[97] Ibid., Vol. 2, p. 230.

The Paths To the Reappearance

The path to the end of suffering is confined to praying for the hastening of the reappearance of the Master of the Age عجل الله تعالى فرجه الشريف in solitude, not mere rolling of the tongue and empty saying of *"hasten the reappearance!"*. Rather, what is important and gives a result is an honest invocation with a sincere intention along with repentance.[98]

Duʿā' al-Faraj

With the reciting of Duʿā' al-Faraj in the time of occultation, every invocation for the hastening of reappearance is meant, such as:

إِلٰهي عَظُمَ الْبَلاءُ

Ilāhī, ʿaẓumal balā'

My God, my afflictions have become enormous[99] [100]

---

[98] Ibid., p. 347.

[99] Majlisī, ʿAllamah Muḥammad Bāqir, *Biḥār al-Anwār*, Vol. 82, p. 206

Fī Riḥāb al-Shaykh Bahjat, Vol. 2, p. 306.

[100] As mentioned previously, his Eminence highly recommended frequent recitation of this Duʿā', which we have added in full to the end of this book.

Repentance And Invocation For the Reappearance

We seek refuge in God from treading upon a path whose condition is to step upon the truth! We seek refuge in God from treading a path we can not return from!

May God make that if we knew that we cannot walk upon this path and must return, we return! Otherwise, God knows how much we must lie and make excuses for our faults!

We hope these events signal the nearing of the Imām of Time عجل الله تعالى فرجه الشريف.

The Master of Command (*Ṣāḥib al-'Amr*), the Imām of Time عجل الله تعالى فرجه الشريف, is more grieved than us that two groups of Muslims have strife among themselves!

History has not before witnessed all this dispute and conflict that exists between Muslims today, which shows that it (sectarianism) is connected to the coming of the Imām عجل الله تعالى فرجه الشريف.

Invocations During the Era of Occultation

They said that in the mausoleum of the Master of Martyrs عليه السلام, a person sat beside a luminous Sayyid who spoke about the reappearance of the Imām of Time عجل الله تعالى فرجه الشريف. Shaykh, with an empty mind and without attention, said,

Some are deniers!

He said,

Yes, by God, he will come and take revenge on them.

Shaykh said,

Will I experience the reappearance?

The veins of the Sayyid turned red, and he said,

If God gives you a lifetime!

There is a secret behind the order to recite this[101] during the occultation:

اللّهمّ عرّفني نفسك

Allāhumma ʿarrifnī nafsak

O God, make me know Yourself

It has also been commanded[102] to read the following invocation,

يا الله يا رحمان يا رحيم، يا مقلب القلوب، ثبت قلبي على دينك

---

[101] The full Duʿāʾ is added in full to the end of this book.

[102] *Fī Riḥāb al-Shaykh Bahjat*, Vol. 1, p. 124.

> *O God, O the Beneficent, O the Merciful, O Turner of hearts, make my heart steadfast upon Your religion*[103]

Duʿāʾ al-Faraj's Results for Those Who Have Wandered Astray

We assumed that supplications for the hastening of reappearance depended upon the supplicant's righteousness, but this is not the case. Even a sinful person should supplicate since the prayers motivate him to leave his sins. But one who continues with his sins will not likely leave them even after the reappearance of the Imām عجل الله تعالى فرجه الشريف!

The reappearance of that Master will be a relief for the believers (not for the evil ones).

If man is drowned in water and mud, how can he be rescued if the world is filled with water?

When his eminence reappears, he will ask,

> Why did you perform this open deed?

It is not certain if he will inquire into hidden deeds.[104]

---

[103] Majlisī, ʿAllamah Muḥammad Bāqir, *Biḥār al-Anwār*, Vol. 52, p. 148.

[104] Ibid., p. 361.

Weeping in Rank

Sayyid Aḥmad Karbalā'ī spent much time in the mosque of Kūfah and al-Sahlah. A person said,

> I saw Sayyid Aḥmad Karbalā'ī in the shrine of Imām al-Mahdī عجل الله تعالى فرجه الشريف worshipping until dawn with tears and cries.[105]

Complete Bond With the Imām!

Obedience and surrender to God after knowing Him results in love for Him as well as those who love Him, such as the Prophets صلوات الله عليهم and the successors عليهم السلام. Among those, Muḥammad صلى الله عليه وآله and the Family of Muḥammad صلوات الله عليهم are the most loved ones by God, and the closest of them to us is his eminence, the Patron of the Age عجل الله تعالى فرجه الشريف.[106]

---

105 *'Ālam al-Ghayb*, p. 372.

106 *Ṣafḥa Min Daftar al-Shams*, p. 155.

The Attentiveness of the Imām عجّل الله تعالى فرجه الشريف Towards the Shīʿah

Imām Jaʿfar aṣ-Ṣādiq عليه السلام said:

من عرف بهذا الأمر ثمّ مات قبل أن يقوم القائم كان له أجر مثل من قتل معه

> Whoever recognizes this matter and then dies before the Qā'im rises will have the reward of one who was martyred alongside him.[107]

A religious doctor, a Shīʿah and believer in guardianship, whom they found in the neighborhood was from among the friends of Imām al-Ḥujjah عجّل الله تعالى فرجه الشريف, wanted to know the names of the companions! One day, he sat alone in his surgery in his own house. A person entered, greeted, sat down, and said,

> Best mister, the companions of Imām al-Ḥujjah عجّل الله تعالى فرجه الشريف are...

and then started hastily going through all their names, one of which he remembered was "Bahrām."

In a few minutes, he mentioned all 313 persons and said,

> These are the companions of al-Mahdī عجّل الله تعالى فرجه الشريف.

And then he stood up, bid farewell, and went!

---

[107] *Muʿjam Aḥadīth al-Imām al-Mahdī* عجّل الله تعالى فرجه الشريف, Vol. 3, p. 402.

The doctor says,

> When he left, I wondered who he was. Was I awake or asleep? I asked my wife in the other room,
>
> > Has anyone had business with me? Has anyone visited me?
>
> She said,
>
> > A person came and spoke swiftly with you!

The doctor says,

> A just realized that I was not asleep and that he was not any ordinary person.[108]

The Green Island

Is the Green Island [*al-Jazīrah al-Khaḍrā'*] a known place? Or is the green island every place where the Master is?

In favor of the second viewpoint is that wherever his eminence, Khaḍir ﷺ, who drank from the water of life, goes, it becomes green! Further, it has been stated regarding Khaḍir ﷺ that he is present wherever he is remembered, and his name is mentioned! Whenever you remember him, greet him as well.

---

[108] *Ṣafḥa Min Daftar al-Shams*, p. 210.

The heart of the believers is the green fresh garden and base of Imām al-Ḥujjah عجل الله تعالى فرجه الشريف.[109]

Those Thirsty For A Bond

Yes; indeed, those thirsty (after the Imām) will be given a cup of union, and those intoxicated by (his) beauty will be given the water of life and wisdom. Considering that the Imām's job is to look after all the needy in the world, is it then possible that we, who are thirsty for wisdom and seek vision and union, will not be given the water we seek?

Special Attentiveness of Imām

In these times, this kind of happenings (special attentiveness of the Imām) seldom occur, if they occur at all! Put the proper is that in a time very close to the reappearance when cruelty will be widespread and

> filled with oppression and tyranny,[110]

it is assumed, or even higher than assumption, that some persons, who remained steady in their faith and took firm steps before the reappearance, will receive special attentiveness to not walk astray from the religion!

---

[109] *Fī Riḥāb al-Shaykh Bahjat*, Vol. 2, p. 308.

[110] Kulaynī, Shaykh Muḥammad b. Yaʿqūb, *al-Kāfī*, Vol. 1, p. 341.

Thus, the Patron of the Age عجل الله تعالى فرجه الشريف supports the people, and the one who has him as his support is a mountain of faith!

It looks like as the time for the reappearance approaches, the people will be filtered and separated (the good from the bad) by the tradition,

> The Imām will come at a time when the majority of those who believed in his Imāmate will have walked astray.

Conversely, those who are victorious in their divine trials will be embraced with special blessings and attentiveness from the Imām عجل الله تعالى فرجه الشريف.

The Support of the Imām of the Age عجل الله تعالى فرجه الشريف

If you are busy in the service of the Imām of Time عجل الله تعالى فرجه الشريف, is it possible that his eminence will not think upon you?[111]

The Imām in the Heart

How many times must we say that the Imām عجل الله تعالى فرجه الشريف has a mosque in the heart of every believer?[112]

---

111 *Bahjat al-ʿĀrifīn*, p. 146.

112 *Mʿālim al-Huda*, p. 90.

Pure Heart

Wherever the Imām عجل الله تعالى فرجه الشريف is, whether on the green island or elsewhere, with him is greenness. And the heart of the believer is the green island. Wherever he (the believer) is, that eminence is as well.

The hearts are dried up from faith and the light of insight. Plant and grow faith and divinity in your hearts so that we may testify that the Imām of Time عجل الله تعالى فرجه الشريف is there.[113]

The Length of Al-Mahdī's عجل الله تعالى فرجه الشريف Government

Perhaps it could be understood from some narrations that the lifetime of Imām al-Ḥujjah عجل الله تعالى فرجه الشريف will not be long after the reappearance. Hence, some who are waiting for him are sad about this!

But they do not think one day with that Master is better than years! Depending upon the yearning of his friends, a thousand years is little still, but they do not realize that one day, with that Master, it has the value of several years for them.[114]

---

113 *Fī Riḥāb al-Shaykh Bahjat*, Vol. 2, p. 179.

114 Ibid., Vol. 2, p. 415.

The Books of Sayyid

It is not good that the people of knowledge do not have the books of Sayyid Ibn Ṭāwūs ⚮. All of his books are good.

Ḥājj Nūrī ⚮ has written the following about Sayyid Ibn Ṭāwūs ⚮:

> The door of encounter with the Occulted One ﷺ was open for him.[115]

---

[115] Ibid., Vol. 2, p. 418.

Nearing the Reappearance

The Prophet ﷺ said:

المهديّ منّا أهل البيت، يصلحه الله في ليلة

> The Mahdī is from us, Ahl al-Bayt. God will prepare him in a single night.[116]

Imām Jaʿfar aṣ-Ṣādiq ؑ said:

إنّ لصاحب هذا الأمرِ بيتا يقال له بيت الحمد. فيه سراج يزهر منذ يوم ولد إلى يوم يقوم بالسيف لا يطفأ

> The master of this affair has a house called 'The House of Praise' (*Bayt al-Hamd*). Inside it, there is a lamp that has been shining since the day he was born until the day he rises with the sword—it will never be extinguished.[117]

Near the Reappearance

One of the people of knowledge said,

> I have an insight in the knowledge of letters. I have used from a verse that the reappearance is close and that Master will come after the year of 1402 A.H (1983 A.D).

---

116 *Muʿjam Aḥadīth al-Imām al-Mahdī* ؑ, Vol. 1, p. 258.

117 Ibid., p. 380.

He even said from which verse he has drawn this conclusion. He also said,

> In my dreams, I saw the Imām of Time ﷺ say,
>
> > In this war—the imposed war of ʿIrāq upon Irān—more bloodshed will be, but do not grieve, I will come myself and sort it out.

The Shīʿah seem mostly afflicted with trials and hardships among all groups and schools.

Reappearance in A Few Steps

Signs (certain as well as possible ones) have been mentioned for that Master's reappearance, but it is not improbable that they would announce that he will come tomorrow (without all of the signs taking place).

The reason for this is that the will of God can be changed concerning the possible signs (so they do not occur), while certain signs might occur at the same time as the reappearance of the Imām ﷺ.

The Reappearance Is Close

Until now, we have given glad tidings to the youths that they will experience the reappearance of the Imām of Time

عجل الله تعالى فرجه الشريف, but now we give glad tidings to the elders as well that they will live to see the reappearance![118]

Hardening of Hearts: A Sign of the Reappearance

Considering that a believer's sorrow and joy are transmitted to other believers, how come we are unaffected by all these calamities and difficulties? Either we do not have faith, or they do! Or our hearts have hardened!

In narrations, it has come that the reappearance of Imām of Time عجل الله تعالى فرجه الشريف will happen

> after the hardening of hearts.[119]

The Time For Reappearance?

Dreams per se are not proof, but along with the Qurʾān and strong proofs, one can trust in them.

A person in the world of dreams saw the Prophet صلى الله عليه وآله sitting in a gathering (*majlis*) surrounded by a group of laymen and clerics.

---

[118] *Ḥadīth-i Viṣāl*, p. 123.

[119] Majlisī, ʿAllamah Muḥammad Bāqir, *Biḥār al-Anwār*, Vol. 51, p. 360.

Fī Riḥāb al-Shaykh Bahjat, Vol. 1, p. 211.

One of them, a cleric, asked,

> When is the reappearance of your son al-Mahdī عجل الله تعالى فرجه الشريف?

His eminence [Prophet Muḥammad صلى الله عليه وآله] answered,

> When will your mosques become like the mosques of Sūrīyah (al-Shām, Syria)?

The cleric asked,

> How are the mosques of Syria?

He answered,

> Their doors are made of gold![120]

From the Signs of Reappearance

One of the signs of the end of time and the rise of al-Mahdī عجل الله تعالى فرجه الشريف is that people's hearts will harden and become like stones!

Anyhow, they have completed the proof (*itmaam al-Ḥujjah*) upon us so that if we know and act upon our obligations in this time, we must throw our hats up in the sky out of joy!

---

[120] During a lesson in Khārij al-Fiqh (Wednesday 28-3-1383 (2004)).

In issues where "innocent until the opposite is proven" is applied, such as accusations of murder, taking possession of peoples' property, honor, Islām, and (performing) the obligations of the religion, we must act with precaution (*ihtiyaat*), i.e., not judge or accuse someone headlong.

Fixing the Time of the Reappearance

In a footnote for a tafsīr of the noble verse

﴿الٓمٓصٓ﴾

﴿*a-l-m-ṣ ('alif lām mīm ṣād)*﴾

﴿*Alif, Lam, Mim, Suad*﴾[121]

in Sayyid Hāshim Bahrānī's ﵀ *Tafsīr al-Burhān* as well as in *Ghāyāt al-Meram*[122] a problematic narration is narrated regarding the time and signs of the reappearance through the counting of letters, which must be analyzed through an intellectual viewpoint. The note's end is written,

> So understand this and hide it from all but those who have an understanding of it.

---

[121] Sūrat al-Aʿrāf, Verse 1.

[122] Majlisī, ʿAllamah Muḥammad Bāqir, *Biḥār al-Anwār*, Vol. 52, p. 106.

Suppose this narration (considering the chain of narrators) is authentic. In that case, one can derive that the tradition that says,

> Those who appoint a time for the reappearance are liars,

does not apply in its absolute sense (in other words, there can be certain situations and conditions where such an appointment does not need to be rejected).

This narration relates the reappearance's month, year, place, and time. This servant has not seen where the year, month, day, and time of the reappearance have been counted and given.

It also tells the narrator about an estimated time from the fall of al-ʿAbbāsiyyūn to the time of their reappearance, which demands great effort if one wants to deduce a desirable conclusion. It says that at such and such a year, al-Umawiyyūn's reign will come to an end.

The narrator says:

> I realized the truth in these words...

If someone strains to interpret this narration, he can even derive the year, month, day, and time. But it demands accuracy, reflection, and logical conclusions.

According to my calculations, I give the probability that it is expected to be between years 1414, 1415, or 1416 in the moon calendar. These years mark the start of the preparations for the reappearance. Similarly to the narration, which stated the year of the end of al-Umawiyyūn's reign, the stated year in reality marked the beginning of the fall, while the actual end was 30 years later.

It has been narrated that one of the scholars who passed away many years ago said:

> The reappearance of the Imām is two 14 next to each other (1414)!

Preparing For the Reappearance

Sufyānī is among the certain conditions for the reappearance, and a couple of hours after the appearance of Sufyānī, Imām will come.

What would we do if they announced that Sufyānī and Imām had appeared? How prepared are we?

There was a scholar in Najaf who had a disciple who was very knowledgeable in the science of arithmancy (*jafr*). He reported events that happened just as he had said. For example, in those days, it was customary for the kings to give titles to the scholars. To one of the scholars, who secretly gave the sultan an amount of lump sugar as a gift to be given a title, he said in a private meeting,

> The efforts with the sugar bits were useless!

while no one was aware of this event! That happened exactly, and that person did not receive any title.

Anyhow, in one of the lessons, he waited until after class, and all the other students had gone, and then told his Master,

> With the science of arithmancy, I can recount the time of the reappearance of Imām! But if I do, you all will rise, run out, and cry out Oh! Oh! Because you can not bear it![123]

The Knowledge of the Imām عجل الله تعالى فرجه الشريف Regarding the Time of His Reappearance

In a narration, it has come that Imām Jaʿfar aṣ-Ṣādiq عليه السلام says,

شيعتنا أصبر منّا... نحن نصبر على ما نعلم،
وهم يصبرون على ما لا يعلمون

[123] During a lesson in Khārij al-Fiqh (Sunday 6-7-1382 (2003)).

> Our followers (Shīʿah) are more patient than us...as we are patient upon what we know while they show patience to what they do not know.

It is amazing what patience the Occulted One عجل الله تعالى فرجه الشريف has, considering that he is aware of all that we know and know not and is conscious of all our affairs, difficulties, and problems.

That Master himself is waiting for the appointed day! And he himself knows when he will arise! What is said regarding his not knowing the reappearance time is incorrect![124]

The Time of Reappearance

They asked a Kirmānshāh (Irān) nobleman about the time of the Imām's عجل الله تعالى فرجه الشريف reappearance. He replied,

> God is the Guide and the Generous One. After the Earth has been filled with oppression and tyranny...

We can not fix what the limit of oppression and injustice is meant by "the Earth has been filled with oppression and tyranny"! But it is apparent that when the oppression is widespread, the time is up and that Master will come, because it was not said "oppression was filled and stayed that way!" but rather "filled." And this decree, that is, "the Earth has been filled with oppression and tyranny," has

---

[124] *Fī Riḥāb al-Shaykh Bahjat*, Vol. 1, p. 210.

been realized in these times in a way that there is no inch on the Earth that is empty of oppression and injustice.

But we can not limit how much is meant with "filled"; hence, all the distinctions of the reappearance have not been realized, and all the signs have not been fulfilled. Thus, we understand that the limit meant by "filled" has not yet been reached.

What tribulations we Muslims have brought upon ourselves, even when the Prophet ﷺ was alive! In that time, when the Prophet ﷺ asked for a pen and paper to write his will, our elders said,

> This man is hallucinating![125]

The Year of Reappearance!

A person said,

> I saw the second caliph in my dreams and asked him,
>
> > In what year will al-Mahdī عجل الله تعالى فرجه الشريف reappear?

What a question! On to what a person!

> He answered,

---

[125] Ibid., Vol. 2, p. 154-155.

> This matter has been mentioned in Sūrat al-Anbiyā'!

That person says,

> We searched the relevant verses to see whether such a thing can be found. We did not find anything but in the verse:

﴿بَلْ تَأْتِيهِم بَغْتَةً﴾

﴿*bal ta'tīhim baghtatan*﴾

﴿*Indeed, it will overtake them suddenly*﴾[126]

We counted the word "sudden" (*baghtatan*) using the science of counting letters (*Abjadiyyah*). The result was 1408 A.H., which had already passed according to the moon calendar.

And if the word "ba, ghayn, ta, ha" (the Arabic letters in the word) is counted with another system of counting letters (*Zubur and Bayyināt*), the result is either just above 1460 or 1470! Even though their difference with the first year (1407) is not that big, we will not even remember the

[126] Sūrat al-Anbiyā', Verse 40.

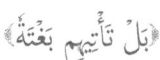

Imām if it will take until 1460 or 1470! We do not have so much endurance![127]

Do You Know

Is it possible that our Master is unaware of us? Or will he abandon us in our condition? If the students (of religion) act upon their obligations, they should not be worried; the Master will be careful of them. It is not so that he will turn away his sight from us.

Traditions in the Era of Reappearance

All our narrations and the sayings of our scholars will remain until the reappearance and even during the days of the reappearance. As that which occurs afterward explains and is a confirmation to what was said before, not a contradiction to it (in other words, what the Imām of Time says and does at the time of reappearance is an explanation to and a confirmation of the previous Imāms' words, and he does not contradict them).

Hence, this matter will remain during the reappearance and be of use.[128]

[127] When it comes to narrated sayings like this, it is essential to consider the element of probability, as His Eminence, Āyatullāh Bahjat, has emphasized multiple times throughout this book.

[128] During a lesson in Khārij al-Fiqh (8-11-1382 (2003)).

The Method of Victory

In the time of the Master of the Age's عجل الله تعالى فرجه الشريف reappearance, it is not certain if everyone will have faith in him out of sincerity, as a great portion will believe in him out of fear for his sword.

He will kill a large number in such a way that a group will say,

> What! Does the son of the Prophet also kill so many people and spill so much blood?[129]

---

[129] During a lesson in Khārij al-Fiqh (Sunday 25-2-1384 / 6 Rabīʿ ath-Thānī 1426 (2005)).

The Honor of Encounters

Imām al-Mahdī عجّل الله تعالى فرجه الشريف said:

ولو أنّ أشياعَنا وفّقهمُ اللهُ لطاعتهِ على اجتماعٍ من القلوبِ في الوفاءِ بالعهدِ عليهم، لما تأخّرَ عنهمُ اليُمنُ بلقائِنا، ولتعجّلتْ لهمُ السعادةُ بمشاهدتِنا على حقّ المعرفةِ وصدقِها منهم بنا. فما يحبسُنا عنهم إلّا ما يتّصلُ بنا ممّا نكرههُ ولا نؤثِرُهُ منهم.

> If our followers (*Shīʿah*)—may God grant them success in His obedience—were truly united in fulfilling the covenant placed upon them with sincere hearts, then the blessing of meeting us would not be delayed for them, and they would swiftly attain the happiness of witnessing us with true knowledge and certainty. But what holds us back from them is nothing but the actions that reach us from them, which we dislike and do not prefer.[130]

Announcing Encounter

Repeatedly informing people about a vision of or a meeting with Imām al-Mahdī عجّل الله تعالى فرجه الشريف is the work of a pretender. And such a claim (will create the illusion) of a pivotal certainty.[131]

---

[130] Ṭabrisī, Shaykh Aḥmad b. ʿAlī Ṭabrisī, *al-Iḥtijāj*, Vol. 2, p. 498.

[131] The writer is saying that frequently recounting an encounter or vision of Imām al-Mahdī عجّل الله تعالى فرجه الشريف will make it seem like a fact among people. This can result in unverified or unverifiable claims being widely accepted as true, creating an illusion of certainty around something lacking real proof.

Claiming Encounter

The narration,

> The one who claims to have seen me...

certainly does not include hearing, sound, and correspondence. If someone claims to have heard the voice of the Imām of the Age عجل الله تعالى فرجه الشريف or received a letter from that Master, he should not be discarded. And even if someone has the honor of meeting that Master and after he has gone realizes it was Imām whom he had met, he should not be rejected.[132]

Seeing the Friend

Shaykh ʿAlī Zāhid قدس سره, who used to go to Masjid al-Sahlah on Tuesday nights, was asked,

> Until now, considering all these times you have gone to Masjid al-Sahlah, have you seen anything so far? Have you had the honor of encountering with the Master of Command (Ṣāḥib al-ʾAmr) عجل الله تعالى فرجه الشريف?

He replied,

> I have not even seen someone whom I might consider to be him!

---

[132] During a lesson in Khārij al-Fiqh (Wednesday 16-7-1382 (2003)).

In this state, he persisted in going (there)![133]

Better than Encounter!

A person does not need to be after and seek an encounter with the Patron of the Age عجّل الله تعالى فرجه الشريف. Rather, perhaps a 2-unit prayer after turning (tawassul) to the Imāms عليهم السلام is better than an encounter! Wherever we are, the Master sees and hears, and worship during occultation is better than worship during presence!

Also, visiting (Ziyārah) of all the pure Imāms عليهم السلام is the same as visiting Imām al-Ḥujjah عجّل الله تعالى فرجه الشريف himself.[134]

Oblivion From His Eminence

Mere finding and seeing that Master is not important; hence, seeing Master in 'Arafah or elsewhere does not always occur. A person said,

> Perhaps you also have encountered that master!

And many have had the honor of encountering it. If you meet that Master, do not tell him to want from God that you are given a wife, a house, healed from this or that personal disease or the like! As these things are not of such importance.

---

[133] *Fī Riḥāb al-Shaykh Bahjat*, Vol. 2, p. 127.

[134] Ibid., Vol. 1, p. 187.

Another person said,

> During seclusion (*i'tikāf*) in Masjid Kūfah, I saw that
> Master in my dreams where he said to me,
>
>> These persons who come here (Masjid Kūfah) are
>> good believers, but all have personal wishes, such as
>> wanting a home, a child, etc., and have come for
>> the fulfillment of that wish. But no one has come
>> for me!

No dreams are needed to realize this. We all are indeed
thinking of our wishes and desires and think not upon that
Master whose benefit returns to and affects everyone,
which is most important![135]

The Way To Encounter

For Ziyārat of the Occulted One عَجّلَ اللّٰهُ تَعَالَى فَرَجَهُ الشَّرِيف, sends many blessings
upon Muḥammad ﷺ and his family عَلَيْهِمُ السَّلَام and give it as a gift
to his holiness, together with praying for the hastening of
his reappearance (*Du'ā' al-Faraj*). Also, go to Masjid
Jamkarān and perform its prayers.[136]

---

[135] Ibid., Vol. 2, p. 26.

[136] *Naḥwa al-Ḥabīb*, p. 59.

Self-Reformation is the Secret to True Honor

Sayyid Qāḍī ☼ taught a seclusion to Shaykh Muḥammad-Taqī al-'Āmilī (the writer of the notes for Sabzawārī's *Sharḥ al-Manẓūma*) so that he would meet Imām.

He started his seclusion in Wādī as-Salām or Masjid al-Sahlah, but the seclusion was not completed, instead, his fright overtook him, and he fled!

Sayyid Qāḍī tells him,

> Do not fear! And why run away?

It was apparent that he was aware of the situation![137]

Reform, the Condition of Encounter

In Tehran, a scholar taught the book of jurisprudence, *Lum'ah*. He heard and saw remarkable things from one of his disciples, who was not very good in his studies. One day, a knife of the scholar he was very attached to and used for sharpening new pens was lost, and as much as he sought, he could not find it. Thinking that his children had taken the knife and lost it, he treated his children and family very harshly and with anger.

---

[137] *'Ālam al-Ghayb*, p. 365.

A time passes like this, and the knife is not found, nor does the anger of the scholar settle!

One day after class, that disciple came forth and, without any foreword, said,

> Mister! You have put your knife in the pocket of your old vest and forgotten it there! What harm have the children done?

The scholar remembers and is surprised how that disciple could have known this! From then on, he is certain that his disciple has some bond with God's friends.

One day, he tells his disciple,

> After class, I want to speak with you.

Once the class is over and everyone has gone, he says,

> Dear one, it is apparent that you are connected somewhere. Tell me, do you have the honor to meet the Imām of Time عجل الله تعالى فرجه الشريف?

He insists, and the disciple has no way but to tell the story of his encounter with Imām. The scholar then says,

> My dear one! Next time you encounter him, send my greetings and ask if it is appropriate that he grant this lowly one the honor of a couple of minutes of the encounter.

Some time passes without the disciple mentioning anything, and the scholar, afraid of the answer being negative, does not dare ask. But because a long time has passed, the scholar's patience runs out, and one day, he asks the disciple,

> Dear one! Is there any news regarding what I asked?

The disciple turns from one side to the other and does not know what to say. His scholar says,

> My dear, do not be shy and narrate what has been said to this lowly servant, because you are only the messenger and 'there is nothing upon the messenger but to deliver the message.'

With great sorrow, that disciple said,

> The Master said,
>
> > It is not necessary that we give a few minutes of meeting. Polish yourself, and I will come myself to you![138]

The Youthful Face of Imām

Those who have had the honor of encountering Imām al-Ḥujjah عجل الله تعالى فرجه الشريف, in reality, or dreams, usually see him in a youthful state with a face aged 30-40 years!

---

[138] *Bahjat al-ʿĀrifīn*, p. 180.

Except for one person, a seeker, who has seen him in the Age of a thousand and something years (that is in his real Age).[139]

Letter On the Command of Imām

Sayyid Qāḍī قدس سره, who was the friend of Sayyid Ḥasan al-Ṣadr قدس سره, said that he (al-Ṣadr) wrote letters on the command of the Patron of the Age عجل الله تعالى فرجه الشريف!

Sayyid Ḥasan al-Ṣadr قدس سره had extensive knowledge in jurisprudence (fiqh).[140]

My Coming Is Close!

Should we not want a person in whom God has laid the reform of society to emerge?

He in Masjid al-Sahlah, Jamkarān, in sleep and wake, has whispered in the ears of his friends without them seeing him,

> My coming is close, pray!

Or according to a saying,

---

[139] Ibid.

[140] *'Ālam al-Ghayb*, p. 371.

> My coming is close; pray that God's will is not changed![141]

Experience the Time of Reappearance

A person connected to the Patron of the Age ﷺ informed me that Imām said the reappearance is close. When the person asked him how close, he answered,

> Sayyid Bahjat will experience the reappearance.[142]

The Attendance of Imām At (Religious) Gatherings

Many times, it has been seen and said that Imām al-Ḥujjah ﷺ is present during gatherings of intercession (*tawassul*) or reciting the Event of the Cloak (*Ḥadīth al-Kisāʾ*), as well as his noble forefather the Prophet ﷺ, ʿAlī ؑ, Fāṭimah ؑ, Ḥasan ؑ and Ḥusayn ؑ are present. The people of the cloak *(ahl al-kisa)* have a higher rank than that Master, but that Master has some virtues and characteristics which they

---

[141] *Fī Riḥāb al-Shaykh Bahjat*, Vol. 1, p. 108.

[142] *Ḥadīth-i Viṣāl*, p. 124.

do not have, such as longevity, and that God's light and bounties currently reach him.[143]

Definite Encounter

Shaykh Ḥajj Ṭāhā Najaf (one of the sources of emulation (Marjaʿ) and contemporary of Ḥasan Shīrāzī) had encounters with the Imām of the Age.[144]

His Eminence in the Gathering of Ḥadīth al-Kisāʾ

A person narrated that he found a copy of Ḥadīth al-Kisāʾ which had as a condition that incense should be lit when reading it!

Whoever reads it fulfilling that condition, Imām al-Ḥujjah, and the light of the five pure ones will be present in that gathering.

It has not gone a year since that person passed away.

---

143 Note: The author's intent in saying "God's light and bounties currently reach him" is that the Imām of each era serves as the recipient of divine light and blessings, which he then conveys to creation. This role is passed down from one Imām to the next. Since the Imām of our time is Imām al-Mahdī, he now holds this responsibility. However, this is not an exclusive trait of his; rather, all previous Imāms also fulfilled this role during their respective times.

144 ʿĀlam al-Ghayb, p. 49.

Shouldn't our attention on God be connected to His minister and friend?[145]

Kūfī Encounter

I have seen Shaykh Muḥammad Kūfī, who had two well-known encounters that do not need any source. One of these has the following story:

He had his residence above his house. He heard a voice from below saying that the Master was in Masjid al-Sahlah, so he went there.

Shaykh Muḥammad is afraid of going to the mosque at night; hence, he does not pay attention. Again, he hears the voice, and his wife tells him to go! Shaykh Muḥammad, with a shiver and quiver, proceeds towards the mosque. Near the mosque, he sees a young Arab with a dagger and is frightened! But the youth smiles at him, and they approach the mosque together. That Arab calls from behind the gate, and the gate opens! They both enter the mosque, each sitting in a corner and worshiping. After some time, Shaykh Muḥammad suddenly realizes they have just unlocked and opened the mosque's gates![146]

---

145 *Fī Riḥāb al-Shaykh Bahjat*, Vol. 1, p. 365.

146 *ʿĀlam al-Ghayb*, p. 54.

The Blessings of Reappearance

They have written: a person in Karbalā' by the shrine of the Master of Martyrs عليه السلام wanted to pray and did not know if it was the night of the 1st of the month of Rajab, which is the night of Ziyārat, the Master of Martyrs عليه السلام, or not. Hence, he asks,

> Is it the night of the 1st of the month of Rajab tonight or not?

Another person who was going to engage in prayers answered,

> Yes, tonight is the night of Ziyārat!

He meant that it was the night of the 1st month of Rajab.

God knows how we would be enriched by and in what ways we would benefit from the Imām of Time's عجل الله تعالى فرجه الشريف presence among us, even in affairs such as finding out the start of the month or when the pure Imāms' عليهم السلام birthdays and death anniversaries will occur.

Encounter in Sleep

A Sayyid, who has encountered the Occulted One عجل الله تعالى فرجه الشريف several times, said,

My three-month-old baby became sick, and the doctor said that serum must be given to her. I refused and instead went to the mosque of Jamkarān and sought intercession (tawassul). I dreamt of that Master sitting at the *miḥrāb*[147], encompassing everyone in his compassion. I stepped forth and said my wish,

> My baby is sick, and until you heal her, I will not leave. Also, I want a house as well as go to Karbalā'!

That Master said,

> Your baby is healed; when you return home, your family will say she is better, and her illness will be gone in the afternoon. A house will also be arranged, and you will go to Karbalā'!

I returned home and saw that my baby was better, and in the afternoon, her illness was gone. A house was arranged; a person gave me a piece of land, another person a building, and another person something else in this manner until the house was completed. And also, I met a builder from Karbalā' and finally went to Karbalā'![148]

---

[147] A miḥrāb is a semicircular niche in the wall of a mosque that indicates the direction of the qiblah (the Ka'bah in Makkah), toward which Muslims face in prayer.

[148] Ibid., p. 53.

The Control of the Imām of the Age عجّل الله تعالى فرجه الشريف

Shouldn't we become conscious that we have a leader who sees our states? Woe upon us if we do not see him as a witness of our deeds and do not view him as a bystander in every place!

Personal sins committed in privacy that do not affect society deserve hell, "except if purified with repentance."

How will then the end of social sins that cause changes and disorder in the society, such as forbidding the permissible or abandoning the obligatory, taking property, tearing apart reverence, killing of pure souls, spilling the blood of Muslims, judging unjustly, etc., etc., be?

With the faith of a leader who is "God's seeing eye," can we flee and hide from divine chastisement and do whatever we desire? What answer will we give?

We are given all the tools and seasonings by him and use them for the benefit of the enemy! And we become puppets in the hands of infidels and strangers and help them! How hard it will be for us if it is not a habit for us to first consider the pleasure and displeasure of that Master in every action we want to perform and do not act in a way to attract his satisfaction and happiness!

Although the satisfaction and discontent of that Master are obvious in all matters, they return to self-evident matters.

Precaution must be taken in matters that are not evident and where doubt pertains.

Recently, a person had doubts about which scholar he should choose as his source of emulation (marjaʿ). In his dreams, the face of a renowned person was presented to him. He went to Najaf and, after searching for that scholar.

Similarly, it has happened for some, regarding if they should remain in their following (*taqlīd*) of a deceased scholar or choose a living one, that they have heard from the graves of the Infallibles, *Remain!*[149]

Encounter in Madīnah

Many people have also encountered that Master in our time. One of the Sayyids of Isfahan went to Madīnah, where he, in a letter, wanted from the Prophet ﷺ to be granted the honor of an encounter with the Imām of the Age عجل الله تعالى فرجه الشريف.

That noble Sayyid said,

> There was no encounter until the last day when I was going to leave Madīnah. In the last hour, when I was making Ziyārat and was going to exit from the shrine through the gate, I saw an illuminated man enter the shrine and in no way being affected by the crowding!

---

[149] *Fī Riḥāb al-Shaykh Bahjat*, Vol. 1, p. 89.

> He entered easily. He greeted me when he reached me and said,
>
> > I am his son! (That is, I am the son of the Prophet).
>
> Afterward, I started pondering who he was, and that was not affected the least by the crowding! And what was it with his greeting and saying? I understood that it was that dignified one I wanted to encounter![150]

The Imām of the Age عجل الله تعالى فرجه الشريف in the Viewpoint of Ahl al-Sunnah

Many scholars of Ahl al-Sunnah, especially the mystics, confess to the Seal of Apostles عجل الله تعالى فرجه الشريف. Even Ṣadr ad-Dīn al-Qūnawī, the disciple of Muḥyī ad-Dīn b. ʿArabī writes in his testament,

> If you experience Imām al-Mahdī عجل الله تعالى فرجه الشريف, get your knowledge from him, do not go ahead of him, and do not listen to anyone else.

Muḥyī ad-Dīn b. ʿArabī himself says,

> During circulating the House of God (Kaʿbah), I saw Muḥammad al- Mahdī عجل الله تعالى فرجه الشريف![151]

---

[150] *ʿĀlam al-Ghayb*, p. 52.

[151] *Fī Riḥāb al-Shaykh Bahjat*, Vol. 2, p. 309.

Duʿāʾ al-Faraj At Its Right Time!

One of the Sayyids, who do not wear the Prophet's ﷺ clothes, signs eulogies and answers religious questions, who recently bought a house near the mosque of Jamkarān and now lives there, has several times seen that Master going into occultation after coming out from the mosque of Jamkarān. But once, when they met while they were speaking, that Master went into occultation.

That Master told him to tell those who recite Duʿāʾ al-Faraj to recite it at the right time![152]

The Mosque of Jamkarān

Some of the pure and good ones have Q&A sessions with the Master of the Command (Ṣāḥib al-ʾAmr) عجل الله تعالى فرجه الشريف, requests for wishes are answered, and hear the voice of that Master in the mosque of Jamkarān!

A person whom I had seen in reality told me in my dreams,

> Why don't you go to the mosque of Jamkarān?[153]

---

[152] *ʿĀlam al-Ghayb*, p. 53.

[153] *Fī Riḥāb al-Shaykh Bahjat*, Vol. 2, p. 86.

Attachment To the Imām

Shaykh Ghulām-Riḍā Kisā'ī was the caretaker of a theological school in Tabriz. He had great morals toward the students and was a pure man who sincerely served the soldiers of the Imām of the Age عجل الله تعالى فرجه الشريف.

One of the students said,

> One night, I came out of my room and saw the little room of this caretaker being illuminated with such a light which can not be compared to ordinary lights! I stepped forward and realized that he was talking with someone! I heard the caretaker's voice but not any sound from the other person. After a while, the illumination went out! I went forth and knocked on the door. The caretaker asked what I wanted. I asked who had been there, but he did not say anything. I said,
>
>> Either tell me, or I will scream and inform all students!
>
> He thought for a while, and even though he talked very little, he said,
>
>> I will tell you if you promise not to narrate to anyone until Friday.
>
> I promised. He then said,

> On Friday, one of the servants (of the Imām) will die, and the Patron of the Age عجل الله تعالى فرجه الشريف has told me that he wants me to replace him! Be prepared on Friday!

This student said,

> That night was Tuesday night. I observed him on Wednesday and Thursday and saw him acting ordinary until Friday. When the sun had risen, I started observing him seriously. At 10 in the morning, he watched his clothes and shoes, then made ablution (wuḍū'), and near noon, he was suddenly gone!
>
> I screamed abruptly, and all the students gathered. I said,
>
>> What happened to Shaykh Ghulām Riḍā?
>
> They said,
>
>> He probably has gone out and will return soon!
>
> I said,
>
>> No! He went without coming back!
>
> And then I narrated the entire story.[154]

[154] *Ḥadīth-i Viṣāl*, p. 120.

The Imām's Plea For Supplication!

A person who regularly goes to the mosque of Jamkarān said,

> I saw the Master in the mosque of Jamkarān. He told me,
>
> > Tell those whose hearts burn for us to pray for us!
>
> Then he suddenly disappeared from my sight, not walking away but slowly disappearing!

The same person dreamt of that Master a week before this.

But alas, everyone goes to the mosque of Jamkarān for the fulfillment of their wishes without knowing how that Master wants them to pray for the hastening of his reappearance!

Similarly, he said to that person,

> These who have come here are our good friends, and all of them have a wish: a house, a wife, children, wealth, religious payments, but no one thinks of me!

Yes, it has been a thousand years now since he was imprisoned. Hence, everyone who goes to a holy place, such as the mosque of Jamkarān, for the fulfillment of his wishes should want the greatest of wishes from God, namely the blessed bond and his reappearance.[155]

The Instruction of Taqlīd

The following story prevailed among the followers of Sayyid Qāḍī ﷫:

A person from India went to Najaf and, in Masjid al-Sahlah, besought (tawassul) the Patron of the Age ﷤ to ask him which scholar he should imitate (taqlīd).

When the encounter happens, the Master shows him a scholar and says,

Follow (do taqlīd of) this person.

Hence, the Indian stays in Najaf to identify that scholar. One day, he encounters Sayyid Qāḍī and realizes that it is the same scholar that the Imām had shown him!

But he is not satisfied with this and says to himself,

I must see if he is aware of this himself!

Sayyid Qāḍī ﷫ tells him,

If you have (religious) questions, ask so you may be given its answer!

---

[155] *Fī Riḥāb al-Shaykh Bahjat*, Vol. 2, p. 118.

The Indian says,

> In India, they have asked that a person wants to marry a non-Muslim. The non-Muslim says,
>
> > I will accept Islām.
>
> Now, is this marriage legitimate or not?[156]

In reply, he mentioned the name of a newspaper in India and said,

> Let him marry her if she proclaimed faith in Islām in that paper!

She was, however, not prepared to do this, and it was discovered that she was not serious about accepting Islām!

It is strange! Sayyid Qāḍī was not even aware of the domestic newspapers; how could he know about a newspaper in India and mention it?[157]

---

[156] Generally, outward declaration of belief in Islām is enough for a marriage to be considered valid. However, the author is highlighting a particular viewpoint that if a person does not truly believe in Islām in their heart, the marriage would be invalid.

[157] *ʿĀlam al-Ghayb*, p. 374.

Waiters of the Reappearance!

Every minute that passes is not replaceable; it has passed away, been lost, and will never return. Oh, if we did not know the house or the door of the house, at least we knew about the street (leading to the house)!

Ḥajj Muḥammad ʿAlī Fashandi قدس سره, during an encounter with the Master of Command (Ṣāḥib al-ʾAmr) عجل الله تعالى فرجه الشريف, says,

> People recite Duʿāʾ Tawassul, are waiting for you and want you and your friends are sad!

The Master عجل الله تعالى فرجه الشريف said,

> Our friends are not sad!

We would at least be among the waiters if we sat down and spoke about when the Occulted One عجل الله تعالى فرجه الشريف would come. They want persons who are only for that Master. Those are waiters of the reappearance who await that Master for God and in God's way, not for their desires and wishes!

Why don't we at least develop a bond with that Master like the Christians who, in times of hardship, have a bond with the Bible?[158]

---

158 *Fī Riḥāb al-Shaykh Bahjat*, Vol. 2, p. 187.

Identity Crisis

Imām al-Ḥujjah عجل الله تعالى فرجه الشريف has said to some who have met him,

> These public schools (during the reign of Shah) are sufficient to lead the children astray from the religion.[159]

[159] Ibid., p. 83.

Duʿāʾ al-Maʿrifah
The Supplication of Knowledge

اللّهمّ عرّفني نفسك فإنّك إن لم تعرّفني نفسك لم أعرف نبيّك،

Allāhumma ʿarrifnī nafsak, fa-inna-ka in lam tuʿarrafnī nafsak lam aʿrif nabiyyak.

O God, make me know Yourself, for if You do not make me know Yourself, I will not know Your Prophet.

اللّهمّ عرّفني نبيّك فإنّك إن لم تعرّفني نبيّك لم أعرف حجّتك،

Allāhumma ʿarrifnī nabiyyak, fa-inna-ka in lam tuʿarrafnī nabiyyak lam aʿrif ḥujjatak.

O God, make me know Your Prophet, for if You do not make me know Your Prophet, I will not know Your Proof.

اللّهمّ عرّفني حجّتك فإنّك إن لم تعرّفني حجّتك ضللت عن ديني

Allāhumma ʿarrifnī ḥujjatak, fa-inna-ka in lam tuʿarrafnī ḥujjatak ḍalaltu ʿan dīnī.

O God, make me know Your Proof, for if You do not make me know Your Proof, I will go astray from my religion.

The Blessed Du‘ā’

His Eminence recommends we recite specifically this blessed Du‘ā’ and ask God عزّ وجلّ to bring us the Possessor of Affairs عجّل الله تعالى فرجه الشريف

دعاء عظم البلاء وبرح الخفاء

Du‘ā’ ‘Aẓumal-Balā’ wa Bariḥal-Khafa’

إِلٰهي عَظُمَ الْبَلاءُ

Ilāhī, ‘aẓumal balā’,

My God, my afflictions have become enormous,

وَبَرِحَ الْخَفاءُ

wa bariḥal khafā’,

the matter has come out,

وَانْكَشَفَ الْغِطاءُ

wan kashafal ghiṭā’,

the veil has been lifted,

وَانْقَطَعَ الرَّجاءُ

wan qaṭaʿar rajāʾ,

hope has been cut off,

وَضاقَتِ الأَرْضُ

wa ḍāqatil arḍu,

the Earth has become narrow [despite its expanse],

وَمُنِعَتِ السَّماءُ

wa muniʿatis samāʾ,

and the heaven's mercy has been withheld,

وأَنْتَ الْمُسْتَعانُ

wa antal mustaʿānu,

and You are my resort,

وَإلَيْكَ الْمُشْتَكى

wa ilaykal mushtakā,

and to You I bring my complaint,

وَعَلَيْكَ الْمُعَوَّلُ فِي الشِّدَّةِ والرَّخاءِ

Wa ʿalaykal muʿawwalu fish shiddati war rakhāʾ!

and on You is my reliance in distress and ease.

اَللّهُمَّ صَلِّ عَلى مُحَمَّد وَآلِ مُحَمَّد

Allāhumma, ṣalli ʿalā Muḥammadin wa āli Muḥammad,

O God, bless Muḥammad and the Family of Muḥammad,

أُولِي الأَمْرِ الَّذينَ فَرَضْتَ عَلَيْنا طاعَتَهُمْ

ūlil amr, alladhīna faraḍta ʿalaynā ṭāʿatahum,

whom You have invested with the authority to command,

وَعَرَّفْتَنا بِذلِكَ مَنْزِلَتَهُمْ

wa ʿarraftanā bi dhālika manzilatahum,

and enjoined us to obey,

فَفَرِّجْ عَنا بِحَقِّهِمْ فَرَجاً عاجِلاً قَرِيباً كَلَمْحِ الْبَصَرِ اَوْ هُوَ اَقْرَبُ

fa farrij ʿannā bi ḥaqqihim farajan ʿājilan, qarīban, ka lamḥil baṣari aw huwa aqrab.

So grant us relief, for their sake, a relief that is early and prompt, like the twinkling of the eye or even quicker!

يا مُحَمَّدُ يا عَلِيُّ يا عَلِيُّ يا مُحَمَّدُ

Yā Muḥammadu yā ʿAlī, yā ʿAlīyu yā Muḥammad,

O Muḥammad! O ʿAlī! O ʿAlī! O Muḥammad!

اِكْفِياني فَإِنَّكُما كافِيانِ

ikfiyānī fa innakumā kāfiyān,

Suffice me! For you are indeed my sufficers.

وَانْصُراني فَإِنَّكُما ناصِرانِ

wanṣurānī fa innakumā nāṣirān!

And help me! For indeed you are my helpers.

يا مَوْلانا يا صاحِبَ الزَّمانِ

Yā mawlānā, yā Ṣāḥibaz Zamān,

O our master, Master of the Era!

الْغَوْثَ الْغَوْثَ الْغَوْثَ

alghawth, alghawth, alghawth!

Help me! Help me! Help me!

أَدْرِكْنِي أَدْرِكْنِي أَدْرِكْنِي

Adriknī, adriknī, adriknī!

Rescue me! Rescue me! Rescue me!

السّاعَةَ السّاعَةَ السّاعَةَ

Assāʿata, assāʿata, assāʿah!

This hour! This hour! This hour!

الْعَجَلَ الْعَجَلَ الْعَجَلَ

Alʿajal, alʿajal, alʿajal!

Make haste! Make haste! Make haste!

يا أَرْحَمَ الرّاحِمِينَ

Yā arḥamar rāḥimīn,

O Most Merciful of the merciful,

بِحَقِّ مُحَمَّدٍ وَآلِهِ الطَّاهِرِينَ

bi ḥaqqi Muhammadin wa ālihiṭ ṭāhirīn!

For the sake of Muḥammad and his immaculate Family!

Duʿāʾ al-ʿAhd

Imām Jaʿfar aṣ-Ṣādiq عليه السلام *narrates that one who recites this supplication for 40 [consecutive] mornings; will be counted amongst the helpers of Imām Muḥammad al-Mahdī* عجل الله تعالى فرجه الشريف

اَللّٰهُمَّ رَبَّ ٱلنُّورِ ٱلْعَظِيمِ

Allāhumma Rabba an-Nūri al-ʿAẓīm

O God, Lord of the Great Light

وَرَبَّ ٱلْكُرْسِيِّ ٱلرَّفِيعِ

wa Rabba al-Kursiyy al-Rafīʿ

And Lord of the Elevated Throne

وَرَبَّ ٱلْبَحْرِ ٱلْمَسْجُورِ

wa Rabba al-Baḥri al-Masjūr

And Lord of the Overflowing Sea

وَمُنْزِلَ ٱلتَّوْرَاةِ وَٱلإِنْجِيلِ وَٱلزَّبُورِ

wa Munzila at-Tawrāh wa al-Injīl wa az-Zabūr

And the Revealer of the Torah, the Gospel, and the Psalms

وَرَبَّ ٱلظِّلِّ وَٱلْحَرُورِ

wa Rabba aẓ-Ẓilli wa al-Ḥarūr

And Lord of the Shade and the Heat

وَمُنْزِلَ ٱلْقُرْآنِ ٱلْعَظِيمِ

wa Munzila al-Qur'āni al-'Aẓīm

And the Revealer of the Great Qur'ān

وَرَبَّ ٱلْمَلاَئِكَةِ ٱلْمُقَرَّبِينَ

wa Rabba al-Malā'ikati al-Muqarrabīn

And Lord of the Near Angels

وَٱلأَنْبِيَاءِ وَٱلْمُرْسَلِينَ

wa al-Anbiyā'i wa al-Mursalīn

And [Lord of] the Prophets and the Messengers

اَللَّهُمَّ إِنِّي أَسْأَلُكَ بِٱسْمِكَ ٱلْكَرِيمِ

Allāhumma innī as'aluka bi-ismika al-Karīm

O God, I ask You by Your Generous Name

وَبِنُورِ وَجْهِكَ ٱلْمُنِيرِ

wa bi-Nūri Wajhika al-Munīr

And by the Light of Your Radiant Face

وَمُلْكِكَ ٱلْقَدِيمِ

wa Mulkika al-Qadīm

And by Your Eternal Sovereignty

يَا حَيُّ يَا قَيُّومُ

Yā Ḥayy Yā Qayyūm

O Ever-Living, O Sustainer

أَسْأَلُكَ بِٱسْمِكَ ٱلَّذِي أَشْرَقَتْ بِهِ ٱلسَّمَاوَاتُ وَٱلأَرَضُونَ

as'aluka bi-ismika alladhī ashraqati bihi as-Samāwātu wa al-Arḍūn

I ask You by Your Name, by which the heavens and the Earths are illuminated

وَبِٱسْمِكَ ٱلَّذِي يَصْلَحُ بِهِ ٱلأَوَّلُونَ وَٱلآخِرُونَ

wa bi-ismika alladhī yaṣluḥu bihi al-Awwalūn wa al-Ākhirūn

And by Your Name, through which the first and the last are rectified

يَا حَيّاً قَبْلَ كُلِّ حَيٍّ

Yā Ḥayyan qabla kulli ḥayyin

O Living One before every living being

وَيَا حَيّاً بَعْدَ كُلِّ حَيٍّ

wa Yā Ḥayyan ba'da kulli ḥayyin

And O Living One after every living being

وَيَا حَيّاً حِينَ لا حَيُّ

wa Yā Ḥayyan ḥīna lā ḥayyu

And O Living One when there was no living being

يَا مُحْيِيَ ٱلْمَوْتَىٰ وَمُمِيتَ ٱلأَحْيَاءِ

Yā Muḥyiya al-Mawtā wa Mumīta al-Aḥyā'

O Giver of Life to the Dead and Causer of Death to the Living

يَا حَيُّ لَا إِلٰهَ إِلَّا أَنْتَ

Yā Ḥayy, lā ilāha illā Anta

O Living One, there is no god but You

اَللّٰهُمَّ بَلِّغْ مَوْلَانَا ٱلْإِمَامَ ٱلْهَادِيَ ٱلْمَهْدِيَّ ٱلْقَائِمَ بِأَمْرِكَ

Allāhumma balligh mawlānā al-Imāma al-Hādī al-Mahdī al-Qā'ima bi-Amrik

O God, convey [our salutations] to our Master, the Imam, the Rightly Guided, the Mahdī, the one who rises by Your command

صَلَوَاتُ ٱللّٰهِ عَلَيْهِ وَعَلَىٰ آبَائِهِ ٱلطَّاهِرِينَ

ṣalawātu Allāhi 'alayhi wa 'alā ābā'ihi aṭ-Ṭāhirīn

May God's blessings be upon him and upon his pure forefathers

عَنْ جَمِيعِ ٱلْمُؤْمِنِينَ وَٱلْمُؤْمِنَاتِ

'an jamī' al-Mu'minīn wa al-Mu'mināt

On behalf of all believing men and women

فِي مَشَارِقِ ٱلْأَرْضِ وَمَغَارِبِهَا

fī mashāriqi al-Arḍi wa maghāribihā

In the East and West of the Earth

سَهْلِهَا وَجَبَلِهَا

sahlihā wa jabalihā

On its plains and its mountains,

وَبَرِّهَا وَبَحْرِهَا

wa barrihā wa baḥrihā

On its land and its seas

وَعَنِّي وَعَنْ وَالِدَيَّ

wa 'annī wa 'an wālidayya

And on behalf of me and my parents

مِنَ ٱلصَّلَوَاتِ زِنَةَ عَرْشِ ٱللَّهِ

mina aṣ-Ṣalawāti zinata 'Arshi Allāh

[May it be] a blessing as weighty as God's Throne

وَمِدَادَ كَلِمَاتِهِ

wa midāda Kalimātih

And as vast as the ink of His words

وَمَا أَحْصَاهُ عِلْمُهُ وَأَحَاطَ بِهِ كِتَابُهُ

wa mā aḥṣāhu 'ilmuhu wa aḥāṭa bihi Kitābuh

And as much as His knowledge encompasses and His book records

اَللّٰهُمَّ إِنِّي أُجَدِّدُ لَهُ فِي صَبِيحَةِ يَوْمِي هٰذَا

Allāhumma innī ujadidu lahu fī ṣabīḥati yawmī hādhā

O God, I renew for him on this morning of mine

وَمَا عِشْتُ مِنْ أَيَّامِي

wa mā 'ishtu min ayyāmī

And for the rest of my days in life

عَهْداً وَعَقْداً وَبَيْعَةً لَهُ فِي عُنُقِي

'ahdan wa 'aqdan wa bay'atan lahu fī 'unuqī

A pledge, a covenant, and an oath of allegiance upon my neck

لا أَحُولُ عنها وَلا أَزُولُ أَبَداً

lā aḥūlu 'anhā wa lā azūlu abadan

From which I shall never turn away nor deviate, ever

اَللَّهُمَّ ٱجْعَلْنِي مِنْ أَنْصَارِهِ

Allāhumma aj'alnī min anṣārih

O God, make me among his supporters

وَأَعْوَانِهِ وَٱلذَّابِّينَ عَنْهُ

wa a'wānihi wa adh-Dhābbīna 'anhu

And his aides and those who defend him

وَٱلْمُسَارِعِينَ إِلَيْهِ فِي قَضَاءِ حَوَائِجِهِ

wa al-musāri'īna ilayhi fī qaḍā'i ḥawā'ijih

And those who hasten to fulfill his needs

وَٱلْمُمْتَثِلِينَ لأَوَامِرِهِ

wa al-mumtathilīna li-awāmirih

And those who obey his commands

وَٱلْمُحَامِينَ عَنْهُ

wa al-muḥāmīna 'anhu

And those who defend him

وَٱلسَّابِقِينَ إِلَىٰ إِرَادَتِهِ

wa as-sābiqīna ilā irādatih

And those who rush to fulfill his will

وَٱلْمُسْتَشْهَدِينَ بَيْنَ يَدَيْهِ

wa al-mustashhidīna bayna yadayh

And those who attain martyrdom before him

اَللَّهُمَّ إِنْ حَالَ بَيْنِي وَبَيْنَهُ ٱلْمَوْتُ ٱلَّذِي جَعَلْتَهُ عَلَىٰ عِبَادِكَ حَتْماً مَقْضِيّاً

Allāhumma in ḥāla baynī wa baynahu al-Mawtu alladhī ja'altahu 'alā 'ibādika ḥatman maqḍiyyā

O God, if death—which You have decreed as an inevitable fate for Your servants—comes between me and him

فَأَخْرِجْنِي مِنْ قَبْرِي مُؤْتَزِراً كَفَنِي

fa-akhrijnī min qabrī mu'taziran kafanī

Then raise me from my grave, wrapped in my shroud

شَاهِراً سَيْفِي

shāhiran sayfī

With my sword unsheathed

مُجَرِّداً قَنَاتِي

mujarridan qanātī

And my spear bared

مُلَبِّياً دَعْوَةَ ٱلدَّاعِي فِي ٱلْحَاضِرِ وَٱلْبَادِي

mulabbiyan da'wata ad-Dā'ī fī al-ḥāḍiri wa al-bādī

Responding to the call of the summoner,
whether in the cities or the deserts

اَللَّهُمَّ أَرِنِي ٱلطَّلْعَةَ ٱلرَّشِيدَةَ

Allāhumma arinī aṭ-Ṭal'ata ar-Rashīda

O God, show me the radiant appearance

وَٱلْغُرَّةَ ٱلْحَمِيدَةَ

wa al-Ghurrata al-Ḥamīda

And the praiseworthy countenance

وَاكْحُلْ نَاظِرِي بِنَظْرَةٍ مِنِّي إِلَيْهِ

wa akḥul nāẓirī binaẓratin minnī ilayh

And enlighten my eyes with a glance toward him

وَعَجِّلْ فَرَجَهُ

wa ʿajjil farajah

And hasten his relief

وَسَهِّلْ مَخْرَجَهُ

wa sahhil makhrajah

And ease his emergence

وَأَوْسِعْ مَنْهَجَهُ

wa awsiʿ manhajah

And expand his path

وَٱسْلُكْ بِي مَحَجَّتَهُ

wa asluk bī maḥajjatah

And set me upon his way

وَأَنْفِذْ أَمْرَهُ

wa anfidh amrah

And carry out his command

وَٱشْدُدْ أَزْرَهُ

wa ashdud azrah

And strengthen his support

وَٱعْمُرِ ٱللَّهُمَّ بِهِ بِلادَكَ

wa aʿmur Allāhumma bihi bilādak

And through him, O God, revive Your lands

وَأَحْيِ بِهِ عِبَادَكَ

wa aḥyi bihi ʿibādak

And revive Your servants through him

فَإِنَّكَ قُلْتَ وَقَوْلُكَ ٱلْحَقُّ:

fa-innaka qulta wa qawluka al-Ḥaqq

For indeed, You have said, and Your word is the truth:

«ظَهَرَ ٱلْفَسَادُ فِي ٱلْبَرِّ وَٱلْبَحْرِ

"ẓahara al-fasādu fī al-barri wa al-baḥr"

"Corruption has appeared in the land and the sea"

بِمَا كَسَبَتْ أَيْدِي ٱلنَّاسِ.»

"ẓahara al-fasādu fī al-barri wa al-baḥr"

"Corruption has appeared in the land and the sea"

فَأَظْهِرِ ٱللَّهُمَّ لَنَا وَلِيَّكَ

fa-aẓhir Allāhumma lanā waliyyak

So, O God, manifest to us Your guardian

وَٱبْنَ بِنْتِ نَبِيِّكَ

wa ibna binti Nabiyyik

And the son of Your Prophet's daughter

ٱلْمُسَمَّىٰ بِٱسْمِ رَسُولِكَ

al-musammā bi-ismi Rasūlik

The one who bears the name of Your Messenger

صَلَّىٰ ٱللَّهُ عَلَيْهِ وَآلِهِ

ṣallā Allāhu ʿalayhi wa ālih

May God send blessings upon him and his family

حَتَّىٰ لا يَظْفَرَ بِشَيْءٍ مِنَ ٱلْبَاطِلِ إِلَّا مَزَّقَهُ

ḥattā lā yaẓfara bishay'in mina al-bāṭili illā mazzaqah

Until he does not come upon any falsehood
except that he tears it apart

وَيُحِقُّ ٱلْحَقَّ وَيُحَقِّقَهُ وَٱجْعَلْهُ

wa yuḥiqqu al-Ḥaqqa wa yuḥaqqiqah wa ajʿalh

And he establishes the truth and confirms it, so make him

اَللّٰهُمَّ مَفْزَعاً لِمَظْلُومِ عِبَادِكَ

Allāhumma mafza'an limaẓlūmi 'ibādik

O God, a refuge for Your oppressed servants

وَنَاصِراً لِمَنْ لا يَجِدُ لَهُ نَاصِراً غَيْرَكَ

wa nāṣiran liman lā yajidu lahu nāṣiran ghayrak

And a helper for the one who finds no helper other than You

وَمُجَدِّداً لِمَا عُطِّلَ مِنْ أَحْكَامِ كِتَابِكَ

wa mujaddidan limā 'uṭṭila min aḥkāmi Kitābak

And a restorer of what has been neglected
from the rulings of Your Book

وَمُشَيِّداً لِمَا وَرَدَ مِنْ أَعْلامِ دِينِكَ وَسُنَنِ نَبِيِّكَ

wa mushayyidan limā warada min aʿlāmī Dīnik wa sunani Nabiyyik

And a reviver of what has been recorded from the signs of Your religion and the traditions of Your Prophet

صَلَّىٰ ٱللَّهُ عَلَيْهِ وآلِهِ وَٱجْعَلْهُ

ṣallā Allāhu ʿalayhi wa ālih

May God send blessings upon him and his family

ٱللَّهُمَّ مِمَّنْ حَصَّنْتَهُ مِنْ بَأْسِ ٱلْمُعْتَدِينَ

wa ajʿalhu Allāhumma mimman ḥaṣṣantahu min baʾsi al-muʿtadīn

And, O God, make him among those You protect from the aggression of the transgressors

اَللّٰهُمَّ وَسُرَّ نَبِيَّكَ مُحَمَّداً

Allāhumma wa surr Nabiyyaka Muḥammadan

O God, bring joy to Your Prophet Muḥammad

صَلَّى ٱللَّهُ عَلَيْهِ وآلِهِ

ṣallā Allāhu ʿalayhi wa ālih

May God send blessings upon him and his family

بِرُؤْيَتِهِ وَمَنْ تَبِعَهُ عَلَىٰ دَعْوَتِهِ

biruʾyatih wa man tabiʿahu ʿalā daʿwatih

Through seeing him, and those who follow him in his call

وَٱرْحَمِ ٱسْتِكَانَتَنَا بَعْدَهُ

wa arḥam istikānatana baʿdah

And have mercy upon our weakness after him

اَللّٰهُمَّ اكْشِفْ هٰذِهِ الْغُمَّةَ عَنْ هٰذِهِ الْأُمَّةِ بِحُضُورِهِ

Allāhumma ikshif hādhihi al-ghummata ʿan hādhihi al-Umma bi-ḥuḍūrih

O God, remove this affliction from this nation through his presence

وَعَجِّلْ لَنَا ظُهُورَهُ

wa ʿajjil lanā ẓuhūrah

And hasten his reappearance for us

«إِنَّهُمْ يَرَوْنَهُ بَعِيداً وَنَرَاهُ قَرِيباً.»

"Innahum yarawnahu baʿīdan wa narāhu qarīban."

"They see it as distant, but We see it as near."

بِرَحْمَتِكَ يَا أَرْحَمَ ٱلرَّاحِمِينَ

bi-Raḥmatika yā Arḥama ar-Rāḥimīn

By Your mercy, O Most Merciful of the Merciful

You may then slap your right thigh with your hand three times and, at each time, say the following:

الْعَجَلَ ٱلْعَجَلَ يَامَوْلَايَ يَا صَاحِبَ ٱلزَّمَانِ

al-'ajala al-'ajala yā mawlāya yā Ṣāḥiba az-Zamān

Hasten, hasten, O my Master, O Master of the Age!

www.ingramcontent.com/pod-product-compliance
Lightning Source LLC
Chambersburg PA
CBHW042316120626
46547CB00022B/2113
* 9 7 8 1 9 5 6 2 7 6 6 0 2 *